THE
TREASURY
OF BIBLE
LISTS

THE TREASURY OF BIBLE LISTS

WILLIAM H. SCHWEINFURTH

MOODY PRESS

CHICAGO

Library of Congress Cataloging-in-Publication Data

Schweinfurth, William H.
    The treasury of Bible lists / by William H. Schweinfurth
        p. cm.
    Rev. ed. of: Treasures of Bible truth. c1942.
    ISBN 0-8024-5221-3
      1. Bible—Indexes. I. Schweinfurth, William H. Treasures
    of Bible truth. II. Title

BS432 .S34 2001
220—dc21

00-052718

1 3 5 7 9 10 8 6 4 2
Printed in the United States of America

CONTENTS

Note to Our Readers	7
Preface	9
1. The Bible	11
2. God	19
3. God's Gifts	37
4. Belief and Faith	57
5. Heaven and Hell	75
6. Eternity and the Resurrection	89
7. Jesus	101
8. Pictures of Jesus	123
9. The Christian Life	139
10. The Christian's Heart	161
11. Prayer	169
12. The Return of Christ	177

NOTE TO OUR READERS

The ultimate impact of any book can be measured by how well the author communicates on a particular subject. The accuracy of the message and its relevance to the reader are also critical elements that distinguish a select group of books from the multitude that are available. Most important, those books that build on the foundation of the Bible, with an overriding goal of glorifying God, are the ones that will be of greatest value to the reader. It is these writings that will stand the test of time.

This group of books, taken from the archives of Moody Press, meets those criteria. They are clear in their presentation and easy to read and apply to your life. At the same time, they do not compromise on substance, while presenting strong arguments that remain relevant to today's readers.

The authors write with elegance and conviction; their passion will inspire you. We have chosen to use the New King James Version of the Bible, which maintains the beauty and grace of the original King James Version while being highly readable in today's language.

This series of books is part of our Life Essentials™ line of products because the books fit so well with Life Essentials' objective: to help the readers stay focused on the essentials of life by keeping God at the center of all they do, grounding them in those truths that build their faith and obedience to the triune God.

We pray that these books will bless and help you in your walk of faith, just as they have done for followers of Jesus Christ in past generations.

THE PUBLISHER

PREFACE

❦

WHEN IT PLEASED GOD TO SAVE ME on January 5, 1916, through the reading of *Pilgrim's Progress*, I immediately had a great desire to read and study the Bible. I began to study the Bible by taking the synthetic Bible study course of the Moody Bible Institute of Chicago. Since then I have read the Bible through twice every year, or more than fifty times, spending much time in prayer as I read and meditated upon God's infallible Word. These meditations and outlines are the results of these twenty-five years of Bible reading and study.

Some of these outlines have appeared in *Moody Monthly* from time to time and in other Christian magazines, and many friends have acknowledged their helpfulness.

In sending forth this volume of almost one hundred outlines on various Bible themes, I pray that they will not only prove a help and inspiration to pastors, evangelists, Bible and Sunday school teachers, leaders of young people's groups, and missionaries on home and foreign fields, but that every Bible-loving Christian will find a blessing in thinking upon these vital topics. As a result of such meditations, may every reader grow in grace and in the knowledge of our Lord and Savior Jesus Christ (2 Peter 3:18) and also be able to pass these messages on to others.

The more we think on these great truths revealed in God's Word, the more we will learn to know Him of whom Moses and the prophets did write, and the more we will rejoice in Him, whom having not seen, we love; in whom, believing, we rejoice. "Unto you therefore which believe he is precious" (1 Peter 2:7 KJV).

PART ONE

THE BIBLE

1. WHO WROTE THE BIBLE?

2. SEVEN REASONS TO STUDY THE BIBLE

3. SYMBOLS OF THE SCRIPTURES

4. THE WORD OF GOD

WHO WROTE THE BIBLE?

"All Scripture is given by inspiration of God, and is profitable."

2 Timothy 3:16

1. GOD THE FATHER

"I have written for him the great things of My law, but they were considered a strange thing." Hosea 8:12

(See also Exodus 31:18.)

2. GOD THE SON

"'Heaven and earth will pass away, but My words will by no means pass away.'" Mark 13:31

(See also John 6:63.)

3. GOD THE HOLY SPIRIT

"'Men and brethren, this Scripture had to be fulfilled, which the Holy Spirit spoke by the mouth of David concerning Judas, who became a guide to those who arrested Jesus.'"

Acts 1:16

(See also Acts 28:25.)

4. HOLY MEN OF GOD: THE PROPHETS

"Holy men of God spoke as they were moved by the Holy Spirit." 2 Peter 1:21

"And the Lord spoke by His servants the prophets."

2 Kings 21:10

(See also Jeremiah 36:1–2; Mark 12:36; Acts 3:21; Luke 1:70; Hebrews 1:1.)

SEVEN REASONS FOR STUDYING THE BIBLE

"Your word I have hidden in my heart, that I might not sin against You."

— Psalm 119:11 —

1. IT IS COMMANDED.

"Be diligent to present yourself approved to God, a worker who does not need to be ashamed, rightly dividing the word of truth." 2 Timothy 2:15

2. IT REVEALS THE WAY OF SALVATION.

"And that from childhood you have known the Holy Scriptures, which are able to make you wise for salvation through faith which is in Christ Jesus." 2 Timothy 3:15

3. IT GIVES ASSURANCE TO THE BELIEVER.

"'My sheep hear My voice, and I know them, and they follow Me. And I give to them eternal life, and they shall never perish; neither shall anyone snatch them out of My hand.'"

John 10:27–28

4. IT IS PROFITABLE.

"All Scripture is given by inspiration of God, and is profitable for doctrine, for reproof, for correction, for instruction in righteousness, that the man of God may be complete, thoroughly equipped for every good work." 2 Timothy 3:16–17

5. IT WILL GIVE GREAT PEACE.

"Great peace have those who love Your law, and nothing causes them to stumble." Psalm 119:165

6. THE BIBLE WILL ENDURE FOREVER.

"But the word of the Lord endures forever. Now this is the word which by the gospel was preached to you." 1 Peter 1:25

(See also Psalm 119:89; Mark 13:31.)

7. THE BIBLE WILL JUDGE MEN IN THE LAST DAY.

"'He who rejects Me, and does not receive My words, has that which judges him—the word that I have spoken will judge him in the last day.'" John 12:48

SYMBOLS OF THE SCRIPTURES

"Your word was to me the joy and rejoicing of my heart."
—Jeremiah 15:16

1. ILLUMINATING LAMP
"Your word is a lamp to my feet and a light to my path."
Psalm 119:105

2. REFINING FIRE
"'Is not My word like a fire?' says the Lord." Jeremiah 23:29

3. BREAKING HAMMER
"'Is not My word . . . like a hammer that breaks the rock in pieces?'" Jeremiah 23:29

4. CLEANSING WATER
"That He might sanctify and cleanse it with the washing of water by the word." Ephesians 5:26

(See also John 15:3.)

5. MILK AND MEAT
"As newborn babes, desire the pure milk of the word, that you may grow thereby." 1 Peter 2:2

(See also Hebrews 5:14.)

6. SWORD
"And take the helmet of salvation, and the sword of the Spirit, which is the word of God." Ephesians 6:17

(See also Hebrews 4:12.)

7. SEED FOR SOWING

"Having been born again, not of corruptible seed but incorruptible, through the word of God which lives and abides forever." 1 Peter 1:23

(See also Psalm 126:6; Matthew 13:19–23.)

THE WORD OF GOD

"I will not forget Your word."

— Psalm 119:16 —

1. THE WORD OF GOD LIVES.

"Having been born again, not of corruptible seed but incorruptible, through the word of God which lives and abides forever." 1 Peter 1:23

2. THE WORD OF GOD ABIDES.

"I have written to you, young men, because you are strong, and the word of God abides in you, and you have overcome the wicked one." 1 John 2:14

3. THE WORD OF GOD PIERCES.

"For the word of God is living and powerful, and sharper than any two-edged sword, piercing even to the division of soul and spirit." Hebrews 4:12

4. THE WORD OF GOD SANCTIFIES.

"'Sanctify them by Your truth. Your word is truth.'" John 17:17

(See also 1 Timothy 4:4–5.)

5. THE WORD OF GOD DISCERNS.

"For the word of God is . . . a discerner of the thoughts and intents of the heart." Hebrews 4:12

6. THE WORD OF GOD WORKS.

"For this reason we also thank God without ceasing, because when you received the word of God which you heard from us, you welcomed it not as the word of men, but as it is in truth, the word of God, which also effectively works in you who believe." 1 Thessalonians 2:13

7. THE WORD OF GOD PREVAILS.

"So the word of God grew mightily and prevailed." Acts 19:20

PART TWO

GOD

1. THE UNSPARING GOD

2. IT PLEASED GOD

3. THE "CALLS" OF GOD

4. OUR GOD

5. THE HAND OF THE LORD (IN THE PSALMS)

6. THE HAND OF THE LORD (IN THE BOOK OF ISAIAH)

7. GOD FOR US

8. THE EVERLASTING ARMS

THE UNSPARING GOD

"For the Lord your God is a consuming fire, a jealous God."
∽ Deuteronomy 4:24 *∽*

1. GOD SPARED NOT THEIR SOUL.
"He made a path for His anger; He did not spare their soul
from death, but gave their life over to the plague." Psalm 78:50
(See also Psalm 78:21–33.)

2. GOD SPARED NOT THE ANGELS THAT SINNED.
"God did not spare the angels who sinned, but cast them
down to hell and delivered them into chains of darkness, to
be reserved for judgment." 2 Peter 2:4

3. GOD SPARED NOT THE ANCIENT WORLD.
"And [God] did not spare the ancient world, but saved Noah,
one of eight people, a preacher of righteousness, bringing in
the flood on the world of the ungodly." 2 Peter 2:5

4. GOD SPARED NOT SODOM AND GOMORRAH.
"And turning the cities of Sodom and Gomorrah into ashes,
condemned them to destruction, making them an example to
those who afterward would live ungodly." 2 Peter 2:6

5. GOD SPARED NOT HIS OWN SON.
"He who did not spare His own Son, but delivered Him up
for us all, how shall He not with Him also freely give us all
things?" Romans 8:32

6. GOD WILL NOT SPARE YOU, UNLESS YOU TAKE HEED.
"For if God did not spare the natural branches, He may not
spare you either." Romans 11:21

7. GOD WILL SPARE YOU, IF YOU BELIEVE.

"'He who believes in Him [Jesus] is not condemned; but he who does not believe is condemned already, because he has not believed in the name of the only begotten Son of God.'"

John 3:18

(See also John 5:24.)

IT PLEASED GOD

"Who works all things according to the counsel of His will."
— Ephesians 1:11 —

1. TO BRUISE HIS OWN SON
"Yet it pleased the Lord to bruise Him; He has put Him to grief." Isaiah 53:10

2. TO MAKE ALL FULLNESS DWELL IN HIM
"For it pleased the Father that in Him [Christ] all the fullness should dwell." Colossians 1:19

3. TO SAVE THOSE WHO BELIEVE
"For since, in the wisdom of God, the world through wisdom did not know God, it pleased God through the foolishness of the message preached to save those who believe." 1 Corinthians 1:21

4. TO REVEAL HIS SON IN SAVED ONES
"But when it pleased God, who separated me from my mother's womb and called me through His grace, to reveal His Son in me, that I might preach Him among the Gentiles." Galatians 1:15–16

5. TO MAKE US ONE IN CHRIST
"But now God has set the members, each one of them, in the body just as He pleased. But now indeed there are many members, yet one body." 1 Corinthians 12:18, 20

6. TO MAKE US HIS PEOPLE
"'For the Lord will not forsake His people, for His great name's sake, because it has pleased the Lord to make you His people.'" 1 Samuel 12:22

7. TO GIVE US RESURRECTION BODIES

"But God gives it a body as He pleases, and to each seed its own body. . . . There is one glory of the sun, another glory of the moon, and another glory of the stars; for one star differs from another star in glory. So also is the resurrection of the dead. The body is sown in corruption, it is raised in incorruption. It is sown in dishonor, it is raised in glory. It is sown in weakness, it is raised in power." 1 Corinthians 15:38, 41–43

THE "CALLS" OF GOD

"He who calls you is faithful."
— 1 Thessalonians 5:24 —

1. GOD CALLS US WITH A HOLY CALLING.

"Who has saved us and called us with a holy calling, not according to our works, but according to His own purpose and grace." 2 Timothy 1:9

2. GOD CALLS US TO BE SAINTS.

"Beloved of God, called to be saints." Romans 1:7

(See also 1 Corinthians 1:2.)

3. GOD CALLS US TO PEACE.

"God has called us to peace." 1 Corinthians 7:15

4. GOD CALLS US TO VIRTUE.

"As His divine power has given to us all things that pertain to life and godliness, through the knowledge of Him who called us by glory and virtue." 2 Peter 1:3

5. GOD CALLS US OUT OF DARKNESS.

"But you are a chosen generation, a royal priesthood, a holy nation, His own special people, that you may proclaim the praises of Him who called you out of darkness" 1 Peter 2:9

(See also Colossians 1:13; Ephesians 5:8.)

6. GOD CALLS US INTO HIS MARVELOUS LIGHT.

"Who called you out of darkness into His marvelous light."

1 Peter 2:9

(See also John 8:12; Romans 13:12.)

7. GOD CALLS US TO HIS ETERNAL GLORY.

"May the God of all grace, who called us to His eternal glory by Christ Jesus, after you have suffered a while, perfect, establish, strengthen, and settle you." 1 Peter 5:10

(See also 1 Thessalonians 2:12.)

OUR GOD

"I am the Lord, and there is no other; there is no God besides Me."
Isaiah 45:5

1. HE IS OUR MAKER.

"Oh come, let us worship and bow down; let us kneel before the Lord our Maker." Psalm 95:6

(See also Job 35:10; 36:3; Proverbs 22:2; Isaiah 17:7.)

2. HE IS OUR SALVATION.

"You have ascended on high, You have led captivity captive; You have received gifts among men, even among the rebellious, that the Lord God might dwell there. Blessed be the Lord, who daily loads us with benefits, the God of our salvation! Selah." Psalm 68:18–19

(See also Psalms 79:9; 85:4.)

3. HE IS OUR SHIELD.

"The Lord is my strength and my shield." Psalm 28:7

(See also Genesis 15:1; Psalms 3:3; 33:20; 59:11; 89:18.)

4. HE IS OUR DEFENSE.

"He only is my rock and salvation; He is my defense; I shall not be greatly moved." Psalm 62:2

(See also Psalms 59:9, 17; 62:6; 94:22.)

5. HE IS OUR HELP.

"Our soul waits for the Lord; He is our help and our shield."
Psalm 33:20

(See also 1 Samuel 7:12; Psalms 28:7; 116:6.)

6. HE IS OUR REFUGE.

"The eternal God is your refuge, and underneath are the ever-lasting arms; He will thrust out the enemy from before you, and will say, 'Destroy!'" Deuteronomy 33:27

(See also 2 Samuel 22:3; Psalms 9:9; 46:1, 7; 59:16; 62:7–8; 91:2, 9.)

7. HE IS OUR DWELLING.

"Lord, You have been our dwelling place in all generations." Psalm 90:1

THE HAND OF THE LORD
(in the Psalms)

"May my meditation be sweet to Him."

Psalm 104:34

1. IT IS A SAVING HAND.
"Show Your marvelous lovingkindness by Your right hand, O You who save those who trust in You from those who rise up against them." Psalm 17:7

(See also Psalms 20:6; 106:10; 138:7.)

2. IT IS AN UPHOLDING HAND.
"The steps of a good man are ordered by the Lord, and He delights in his way. Though he fall, he shall not be utterly cast down; for the Lord upholds him with His hand." Psalm 37:23–24

(See also Psalms 18:35; 63:8; 73:23.)

3. IT IS A SEARCHING HAND.
"Your hand will find all Your enemies; Your right hand will find those who hate You." Psalm 21:8

4. IT IS A CHASTENING HAND.
"For day and night Your hand was heavy upon me; my vitality was turned into the drought of summer." Psalm 32:4

(See also Psalms 38:2; 39:10.)

5. IT IS A DELIVERING HAND.
"How You drove out the nations with Your hand, but them You planted; how You afflicted the peoples, and cast them out. For they did not gain possession of the land by their own sword, nor did their own arm save them; but it was Your right hand, Your arm, and the light of Your countenance, because You favored them." Psalm 44:2–3

(See also Psalm 144:7–11.)

6. IT IS A RIGHTEOUS HAND.

"Your right hand is full of righteousness." Psalm 48:10

7. IT IS A JUDGING HAND.

"For in the hand of the Lord there is a cup, and the wine is red; it is fully mixed, and He pours it out; surely its dregs shall all the wicked of the earth drain and drink down."

Psalm 75:8

8. IT IS A CREATING HAND.

"In His hand are the deep places of the earth; the heights of the hills are His also. The sea is His, for He made it; and His hands formed the dry land." Psalm 95:4–5

(See also Psalm 119:73.)

9. IT IS A VICTORIOUS HAND.

"Oh, sing to the Lord a new song! For He has done marvelous things; His right hand and His holy arm have gained Him the victory." Psalm 98:1

10. IT IS A SUPPLYING HAND.

What You give them they gather in; You open Your hand, they are filled with good." Psalm 104:28

11. IT IS A HELPING HAND.

"Let Your hand become my help, for I have chosen Your precepts." Psalm 119:173

12. IT IS A LEADING HAND.

"Even there Your hand shall lead me, and Your right hand shall hold me." Psalm 139:10

THE HAND OF THE LORD
(in the Book of Isaiah)

"Consider the operation of His hands."
— Isaiah 5:12 —

1. IT IS A SMITING HAND.
"Therefore the anger of the Lord is aroused against His people; He has stretched out His hand against them and stricken them." Isaiah 5:25

2. IT IS A STRONG HAND.
"For the Lord spoke thus to me with a strong hand, and instructed me that I should not walk in the way of this people." Isaiah 8:11

3. IT IS A CHASTENING HAND.
"For all this His anger is not turned away, but His hand is stretched out still." Isaiah 9:12, 21

(See also Isaiah 10:4; 14:26.)

4. IT IS A SHAKING HAND.
"In that day Egypt will be like women, and will be afraid and fear because of the waving of the hand of the Lord of hosts, which He waves over it." Isaiah 19:16

5. IT IS A DELIVERING HAND.
"'Indeed before the day was, I am He; and there is no one who can deliver out of My hand; I work, and who will reverse it?'"
Isaiah 43:13

6. IT IS A CREATING HAND.
"'I have made the earth, and created man on it. It was I— My hands that stretched out the heavens, and all their host I have commanded.'" Isaiah 45:12

(See also Isaiah 48:13; 64:8.)

7. IT IS AN INSCRIBING HAND.

"'See, I have inscribed you on the palms of My hands; your walls are continually before Me.'" Isaiah 49:16

8. IT IS A LIFTED HAND.

"Thus says the Lord God: 'Behold, I will lift My hand in an oath to the nations, and set up My standard for the peoples; they shall bring your sons in their arms, and your daughters shall be carried on their shoulders.'" Isaiah 49:22

9. IT IS A COVERING HAND.

"'And I have put My words in your mouth; I have covered you with the shadow of My hand, that I may plant the heavens, lay the foundations of the earth, and say to Zion, "You are My people.'" Isaiah 51:16

10. IT IS A SAVING HAND.

"Behold, the Lord's hand is not shortened, that it cannot save; nor His ear heavy, that it cannot hear. But your iniquities have separated you from your God; and your sins have hidden His face from you, so that He will not hear." Isaiah 59:1–2

11. IT IS A GLORIOUS HAND.

"You shall also be a crown of glory in the hand of the Lord, and a royal diadem in the hand of your God." Isaiah 62:3

12. IT IS A SPREADING HAND.

"'I have stretched out My hands all day long to a rebellious people, who walk in a way that is not good, according to their own thoughts.'" Isaiah 65:2

GOD FOR US

"If God is for us, who can be against us?"
~ Romans 8:31 ~

1. GOD HAS LOVED US.
"Our Lord Jesus Christ Himself, and our God and Father,
who has loved us." 2 Thessalonians 2:16

(See also John 3:16; Romans 5:8; 1 John 4:9.)

2. GOD HAS CALLED US.
"Even us whom He called, not of the Jews only, but also of
the Gentiles." Romans 9:24

(See also 1 Corinthians 7:15; 1 Peter 2:9).

3. GOD HAS BEGOTTEN US.
"Blessed be the God and Father of our Lord Jesus Christ, who
according to His abundant mercy has begotten us again to a
living hope through the resurrection of Jesus Christ from the
dead." 1 Peter 1:3

(See also 1 Peter 1:23; 1 John 5:1.)

4. GOD HAS MADE US ALIVE.
"And you, being dead in your trespasses and the uncircumci-
sion of your flesh, He has made alive together with Him,
having forgiven you all trespasses." Colossians 2:13

(See also Ephesians 2:1, 5.)

5. GOD HAS RECONCILED US.
"Now all things are of God, who has reconciled us to
Himself through Jesus Christ." 2 Corinthians 5:18

(See also Romans 5:10; 2 Corinthians 5:20; Colossians 1:21.)

6. GOD HAS REDEEMED US.
"Christ has redeemed us from the curse of the law, having

become a curse for us (for it is written, 'Cursed is everyone who hangs on a tree')." Galatians 3:13

(See also 1 Peter 1:18; Revelation 5:9.)

7. GOD HAS DELIVERED US.
"He has delivered us from the power of darkness."

Colossians 1:13

(See also 2 Corinthians 1:10; 1 Thessalonians 1:10.)

8. GOD HAS SAVED US.
"Who has saved us and called us with a holy calling, not according to our works, but according to His own purpose and grace which was given to us in Christ Jesus before time began."

2 Timothy 1:9

9. GOD HAS GIVEN US ETERNAL LIFE.
"And this is the testimony: that God has given us eternal life, and this life is in His Son." 1 John 5:11

(See also Romans 6:23.)

10. GOD HAS ANOINTED US.
"Now He who establishes us with you in Christ and has anointed us is God." 2 Corinthians 1:21

(See also 1 John 2:27.)

11. GOD HAS SEALED US.
"In whom also, having believed, you were sealed with the Holy Spirit of promise, who is the guarantee of our inheritance until the redemption of the purchased possession, to the praise of His glory." Ephesians 1:13–14

(See also 2 Corinthians 1:22; Ephesians 4:30).

12. GOD HAS COMMITTED TO US THE WORD.
"God was in Christ reconciling the world to Himself, not imputing their trespasses to them, and has committed to us the word of reconciliation." 2 Corinthians 5:19

THE EVERLASTING ARMS

"Underneath are the everlasting arms."
— Deuteronomy 33:27 —

1. THE ARMS OF EVERLASTING POWER
"'Ah, Lord God! Behold, You have made the heavens and the earth by Your great power and outstretched arm. There is nothing too hard for You.'" Jeremiah 32:17

(See also Jeremiah 27:5; Luke 1:51.)

2. THE ARMS OF EVERLASTING SALVATION
"The Lord has made bare His holy arm in the eyes of all the nations; and all the ends of the earth shall see the salvation of our God." Isaiah 52:10

(See also Isaiah 45:17.)

3. THE ARMS OF EVERLASTING REDEMPTION
"You have with Your arm redeemed Your people." Psalm 77:15

(See also Exodus 6:6; Acts 13:17.)

4. THE ARMS OF EVERLASTING PROTECTION
"Fear and dread will fall on them; by the greatness of Your arm they will be as still as a stone, till Your people pass over, O Lord . . . whom You have purchased." Exodus 15:16

5. THE ARMS OF EVERLASTING SOVEREIGNTY
"'As I live,' says the Lord God, 'surely with a mighty hand, with an outstretched arm, and with fury poured out, I will rule over you.'" Ezekiel 20:33

(See also Isaiah 40:10; Psalm 99:1.)

6. THE ARMS OF EVERLASTING JUDGMENT

"'My righteousness is near, My salvation has gone forth, and My arms will judge the peoples.'" Isaiah 51:5

(See also Jeremiah 21:5.)

7. THE ARMS OF EVERLASTING VICTORY

"Oh, sing to the Lord a new song! For He has done marvelous things; His right hand and His holy arm have gained Him the victory." Psalm 98:1

(See also 1 Corinthians 15:57; 1 John 5:4.)

PART THREE

GOD'S GIFTS

1. ABOUNDING GRACE

2. THE ABUNDANCE OF GOD'S GRACE

3. PEACE

4. OUR GLORIOUS INHERITANCE

5. INCORRUPTIBLE THINGS

6. MARVELOUS THINGS

7. THE RICHES OF GOD IN EPHESIANS

8. PARTAKERS

9. WHAT GOD HAS GIVEN BELIEVERS

ABOUNDING GRACE

"For you know the grace of our Lord Jesus Christ."

2 Corinthians 8:9

1. ABOUNDING GRACE
"But where sin abounded, grace abounded much more. "

Romans 5:20

(See also Romans 5:17; 2 Corinthians 4:15; 9:7–8; James 4:6.)

2. ELECTING GRACE
"Even so then, at this present time there is a remnant according to the election of grace." Romans 11:5

(See also 2 Timothy 1:9.)

3. SAVING GRACE
"For by grace you have been saved through faith, and that not of yourselves; it is the gift of God." Ephesians 2:8

(See also Titus 2:11.)

4. JUSTIFYING GRACE
"Being justified freely by His grace through the redemption that is in Christ Jesus." Romans 3:24

(See also Titus 3:7.)

5. ESTABLISHING GRACE
Do not be carried about with various and strange doctrines. For it is good that the heart be established by grace." Hebrews 13:9

6. SUSTAINING GRACE
"And He said to me, 'My grace is sufficient for you, for My strength is made perfect in weakness.' Therefore most gladly I will rather boast in my infirmities, that the power of Christ may rest upon me." 2 Corinthians 12:9

(See also 1 Peter 5:10.)

7. REIGNING GRACE

"That as sin reigned in death, even so grace might reign through righteousness to eternal life through Jesus Christ our Lord." Romans 5:21

THE ABUNDANCE OF GOD'S GRACE

"And He said to me, 'My grace is sufficient for you.'"
2 CORINTHIANS 12:9

1. ABUNDANT PARDON
"Let the wicked forsake his way, and the unrighteous man his thoughts; let him return to the Lord, and He will have mercy on him; and to our God, for He will abundantly pardon."
Isaiah 55:7

2. ABUNDANT LIFE
"'The thief does not come except to steal, and to kill, and to destroy. I have come that they may have life, and that they have it more abundantly.'" John 10:10

3. ABUNDANT BLESSING
"Now to Him who is able to do exceedingly abundantly above all that we ask or think, according to the power that works in us." Ephesians 3:20
(See also John 16:24.)

4. ABUNDANT PEACE
"'Behold, I will bring it health and healing; I will heal them and reveal to them the abundance of peace and truth.'"
Jeremiah 33:6
(See also Isaiah 26:3; Philippians 4:6–7.)

5. ABUNDANT JOY
"That your rejoicing for me may be more abundant in Jesus Christ by my coming to you again." Philippians 1:26

6. ABUNDANT GRACE

"For all things are for your sakes, that, having spread grace, through the thanksgiving many cause to abound to the glory of God." 2 Corinthians 4:15

7. ABUNDANT ENTRANCE

"For so an entrance will be supplied to you abundantly into the everlasting kingdom of our Lord and Savior Jesus Christ."

2 Peter 1:11

PEACE

"Now may the God of hope fill you with all joy and peace in believing."
— Romans 15:13 —

1. PEACE MISSING

"'There is no peace,' says the Lord, 'for the wicked.'"

Isaiah 48:22

(See also Isaiah 57:20–21.)

2. PEACE PREACHED

"And He came and preached peace to you who were afar off and to those who were near." Ephesians 2:17

(See also Acts 10:36.)

3. PEACE MADE

"By Him to reconcile all things to Himself; . . . having made peace through the blood of His cross." Colossians 1:20

(See also Ephesians 2:14–15.)

4. PEACE GIVEN

"'Peace I leave with you, My peace I give to you; not as the world gives do I give to you. Let not your heart be troubled, neither let it be afraid.'" John 14:27

5. PEACE POSSESSED

"Therefore, having been justified by faith, we have peace with God through our Lord Jesus Christ." Romans 5:1

6. PERFECT PEACE

"You will keep him in perfect peace, whose mind is stayed on You, because he trusts in You." Isaiah 26:3

7. ABUNDANT PEACE

"Be anxious for nothing, but in everything by prayer and supplication, with thanksgiving, let your requests be made known to God; and the peace of God, which surpasses all understanding, will guard your hearts and minds through Christ Jesus." Philippians 4:6–7

OUR GLORIOUS INHERITANCE

"And if children, then heirs—heirs of God and joint heirs with Christ."
— Romans 8:17 —

1. IT IS GIVEN.

"'And now, brethren, I commend you to God and to the word of His grace, which is able to build you up and give you an inheritance among all those who are sanctified.'" Acts 20:32

2. IT IS RECEIVED BY FAITH.

"'To open their eyes, and to turn them from darkness to light, and from the power of Satan to God, that they may receive forgiveness of sins and an inheritance among those who are sanctified by faith in Me.'" Acts 26:18

3. IT IS IN CHRIST.

"In [Christ] also we have obtained an inheritance, being predestined according to the purpose of Him who works all things according the counsel of His will." Ephesians 1:11

4. IT IS GUARANTEED BY THE SPIRIT.

"In Him you also trusted, after you heard the word of truth, the gospel of your salvation; in whom also, having believed, you were sealed with that Holy Spirit of promise, who is the guarantee of our inheritance." Ephesians 1:13–14

5. IT IS GLORIOUS.

"The eyes of your understanding being enlightened; that you may know what is the hope of His calling, what are the riches of the glory of His inheritance in the saints." Ephesians 1:18

6. IT IS ETERNAL.

"And for this reason He is the Mediator of the new covenant, by means of death, for the redemption of the transgressions under the first covenant, that those who are called may receive the promise of the eternal inheritance." Hebrews 9:15

7. IT IS SURE AND SAFE.

"Blessed be the God and Father of our Lord Jesus Christ, who according to His abundant mercy has begotten us again to a living hope through the resurrection of Jesus Christ from the dead, to an inheritance incorruptible and undefiled and that does not fade away, reserved in heaven for you." 1 Peter 1:3–4

INCORRUPTIBLE THINGS

"You were not redeemed with corruptible things."
— 1 Peter 1:18 —

1. THE INCORRUPTIBLE GOD
"Professing to be wise, they became fools, and changed the glory of the incorruptible God into an image made like corruptible man—and birds and four-footed beasts and creeping things." Romans 1:22–23

2. THE INCORRUPTIBLE WORD
"Having been born again, not of corruptible seed but incorruptible, through the word of God which lives and abides forever." 1 Peter 1:23

3. THE INCORRUPTIBLE ORNAMENT
"But let it be the hidden person of the heart, with the incorruptible ornament of a gentle and quiet spirit, which is very precious in the sight of God." 1 Peter 3:4

4. THE INCORRUPTIBLE LOVE
"Grace be with all those who love our Lord Jesus Christ in sincerity." Ephesians 6:24

5. THE INCORRUPTIBLE AND IMPERISHABLE CROWN
"And everyone who competes for the prize is temperate in all things. Now they do it to obtain a perishable crown, but we an imperishable one." 1 Corinthians 9:25

6. THE INCORRUPTIBLE INHERITANCE
"Blessed be the God and Father of our Lord Jesus Christ, who according to His abundant mercy has begotten us again to a living hope through the resurrection of Jesus Christ from the

dead, to an inheritance incorruptible and undefiled and that does not fade away, reserved in heaven for you." 1 Peter 1:3–4

7. THE INCORRUPTIBLE BODY

"Behold, I tell you a mystery: We shall not all sleep, but we shall all be changed—in a moment, in the twinkling of an eye, at the last trumpet. For the trumpet will sound, and the dead will be raised incorruptible, and we shall be changed."

1 Corinthians 15:51–52

MARVELOUS THINGS

"He has done marvelous things."
Psalm 98:1

1. HE HAS CREATED A MARVELOUS UNIVERSE.
"The heavens declare the glory of God; and the firmament shows His handiwork." Psalm 19:1

(See also Hebrews 1:2, 10.)

2. HE HAS INSPIRED A MARVELOUS BOOK.
"All Scripture is given by inspiration of God, and is profitable for doctrine, for reproof, for correction, for instruction in righteousness, that the man of God may be complete, thoroughly equipped for every good work." 2 Timothy 3:16–17

(See also Joshua 1:8; 2 Peter 1:21.)

3. HE HAS BEGOTTEN A MARVELOUS SON.
"In this the love of God was manifested toward us, that God has sent his only begotten Son into the world, that we might live through Him." 1 John 4:9

(See also Psalm 2:7; John 3:16; 1:14, 18; Acts 13:33; Hebrews 1:5; 5:5.)

4. HE HAS ORDAINED HIS SON A MARVELOUS SAVIOR.
"Knowing that you were not redeemed with corruptible things, like silver or gold . . . but with the precious blood of Christ, as of a lamb without blemish and without spot. He indeed was foreordained before the foundation of the world, but was manifest in these last times for you." 1 Peter 1:18–20

(See also Matthew 1:21; 28:6; Luke 19:10.)

5. HE HAS GIVEN HIS SON MARVELOUS AUTHORITY.
"Then Jesus came and spoke to them, saying, 'All authority

has been given to Me in heaven and on earth.'" Matthew 28:18

(See also John 13:3.)

6. HE HAS SENT THE HOLY SPIRIT INTO OUR HEARTS IN A MARVELOUS WAY.

"And because you are sons, God has sent forth the Spirit of
His Son into your hearts, crying out, 'Abba, Father!'"

Galatians 4:6

(See also Romans 8:15–16.)

7. HE HAS WROUGHT A MARVELOUS CHANGE.

"Therefore if anyone is in Christ, he is a new creation; old
things have passed away; behold, all things have become
new." 2 Corinthians 5:17

(See also 2 Corinthians 3:18.)

8. HE HAS PROMISED A MARVELOUS RESURRECTION.

"'Do not marvel not at this; for the hour is coming in which
all who are in the graves will hear His voice and come
forth—those who have done good, to the resurrection of life,
and those who have done evil, to the resurrection of condemnation." John 5:28–29

9. HE HAS PREPARED A MARVELOUS HOME.

"'In My Father's house are many mansions; if it were not so, I
would have told you. I go to prepare a place for you. And if I
go and prepare a place for you, I will come again and receive
you to Myself; that where I am, there you may be also.'"

John 14:2–3

(See also Hebrews 11:16.)

10. HE HAS FORETOLD A MARVELOUS REWARD.

"'Be faithful until death, and I will give you the crown of life.'"

Revelation 2:10

(See also 2 Timothy 4:8; Revelation 22:12.)

THE RICHES OF GOD IN EPHESIANS

"Blessed be the God and Father of our Lord Jesus Christ."
— Ephesians 1:3 —

1. CHOSEN ACCORDING TO GOD'S PLAN
"Who has blessed us with every spiritual blessing in the heavenly places in Christ, just as He chose us in Him before the foundation of the world, that we should be holy and without blame before Him in love." Ephesians 1:3–4

2. ADOPTED ACCORDING TO GOD'S WILL
"Having predestined us to the adoption as sons by Jesus Christ to Himself, according to the good pleasure of His will." Ephesians 1:5

3. REDEEMED ACCORDING TO GOD'S GRACE
"In Him we have redemption through His blood, the forgiveness of sins, according to the riches of His grace." Ephesians 1:7

4. ENLIGHTENED ACCORDING TO GOD'S PLEASURE
"Having made known to us the mystery of His will, according to His good pleasure which He purposed in Himself."
Ephesians 1:9

5. PREDESTINED ACCORDING TO GOD'S COUNSEL
"In whom also we have obtained an inheritance, being predestined according to the purpose of Him who works all things according to the counsel of His will." Ephesians 1:11

6. EMPOWERED ACCORDING TO GOD'S POWER

"And what is the exceeding greatness of His power toward us who believe, according to the working of His mighty power."

Ephesians 1:19

7. STRENGTHENED ACCORDING TO GOD'S GLORY

"That He would grant you, according to the riches of His glory, to be strengthened with might through His Spirit in the inner man." Ephesians 3:16

PARTAKERS

"Heirs of God and joint heirs with Christ."
— Romans 8:17 —

1. THE BELIEVER IS A PARTAKER OF THE HEAVENLY CALLING.

"Therefore, holy brethren, partakers of the heavenly calling, consider the Apostle and High Priest of our confession, Christ Jesus." Hebrews 3:1

(See also Romans 8:30; 9:24; 1 Peter 1:15.)

2. THE BELIEVER IS A PARTAKER OF CHRIST.

"For we have become partakers of Christ if we hold the beginning of our confidence steadfast to the end."

Hebrews 3:14

3. THE BELIEVER IS A PARTAKER OF HIS HOLINESS.

"For they indeed for a few days chastened us as seemed best to them, but He for our profit, that we may be partakers of His holiness." Hebrews 12:10

4. THE BELIEVER IS A PARTAKER OF HIS SUFFERINGS.

"Beloved, do not think it strange concerning the fiery trial which is to try you, as though some strange thing happened to you; but rejoice to the extent that you partake of Christ's sufferings, that when His glory is revealed, you may also be glad with exceeding joy." 1 Peter 4:12–13

(See also Romans 8:17; 2 Corinthians 1:7.)

5. THE BELIEVER IS A PARTAKER OF HIS PROMISE.

"That the Gentiles should be fellow heirs, of the same body, and partakers of His promise in Christ through the gospel."

Ephesians 3:6

(See also Galatians 4:28.)

6. THE BELIEVER IS A PARTAKER OF THE DIVINE NATURE.

"By which have been given to us exceedingly great and precious promises, that through these you may be partakers of the divine nature, having escaped the corruption that is in the world through lust." 2 Peter 1:4

7. THE BELIEVER IS A PARTAKER OF THE INHERITANCE.

"Giving thanks to the Father who has qualified us to be partakers of the inheritance of the saints in the light."

Colossians 1:12

(See also 1 Peter 1:3–5.)

WHAT GOD HAS GIVEN BELIEVERS

"Every good gift . . . comes down from the Father of lights."
~ James 1:17 ~

1. ETERNAL LIFE

"And this is the testimony: that God has given us eternal life, and this life is in His Son. He who has the Son has life; he who does not have the Son of God does not have life."

1 John 5:11–12

(See also John 20:31; Romans 6:23.)

2. HOLY SPIRIT

"Now He who establishes us . . . in Christ and has anointed us is God, who also has given us . . . the Spirit."

2 Corinthians 1:21–22

(See also Acts 5:32; 1 Thessalonians 4:8; 1 John 4:13.)

3. ASSURANCE

"Because He has appointed a day on which He will judge the world in righteousness by the Man whom he has ordained. He has given assurance of this to all by raising Him from the dead." Acts 17:31

(See also Romans 8:29–39; John 10:27–30).

4. UNDERSTANDING

"And we know that the Son of God has come and has given us an understanding, that we may know Him who is true; and we are in Him who is true, in His Son Jesus Christ. This is the true God and eternal life." 1 John 5:20

5. ALL THINGS THAT PERTAIN TO LIFE AND GODLINESS

"His divine power has given to us all things that pertain to life and godliness, through the knowledge of Him who called us by glory and virtue." 2 Peter 1:3

6. EVERLASTING CONSOLATION AND GOOD HOPE

"Now may our Lord Jesus Christ Himself, and our God and Father, who has loved us and given us everlasting consolation and good hope by grace, comfort your hearts and establish you in every good word and work." 2 Thessalonians 2:16–17

7. THE MINISTRY OF RECONCILIATION

"Now all things are of God, who has reconciled us to Himself through Jesus Christ, and has given us the ministry of reconciliation." 2 Corinthians 5:18

PART FOUR

BELIEF AND FAITH

1. THOSE WHO SEEK THE LORD

2. THOSE WHO BELIEVE

3. THE GLORIOUS RESULTS OF FAITH

4. THE GOSPEL

5. WHY YOU SHOULD BE SAVED

6. THE GREAT CHRISTMAS MESSAGE

7. THE BELIEVER IS JUSTIFIED

8. COMPLETENESS IN CHRIST

9. WHOEVER BELIEVES

THOSE WHO SEEK THE LORD

"Seek the Lord while He may be found, call upon Him while He is near."
— Isaiah 55:6 —

❧

1. THEY SHALL FIND GOD AND LIVE.
"And you will seek Me and find Me, when you search for Me
with all your heart." Jeremiah 29:13

(See also Deuteronomy 4:29; Amos 5:4.)

2. THEY SHALL REJOICE.
"Glory in His holy name; let the hearts of those rejoice who
seek the Lord." Psalm 105:3

(See also Psalms 40:16; 70:4.)

3. THEY SHALL UNDERSTAND.
"Evil men do not understand justice, but those who seek the
Lord understand all." Proverbs 28:5

4. THEY SHALL NOT LACK.
"The young lions lack and suffer hunger; but those who seek
the Lord shall not lack any good thing." Psalm 34:10

5. THEY SHALL NOT BE CONFOUNDED.
"Let not those who wait for You, O Lord God of hosts, be
ashamed because of me; let not those who seek You be
confounded because of me, O God of Israel." Psalm 69:6

6. THEY SHALL NOT BE FORSAKEN.
"And those who know Your name will put their trust in You;
for You, Lord, have not forsaken those who seek You."

Psalm 9:10

7. THEY SHALL BE BLESSED.

"'The hand of our God is upon all those for good who seek Him, but His power and His wrath are against all those who forsake Him.'" Ezra 8:22

8. THEY SHALL BE GREATLY REWARDED.

"But without faith it is impossible to please Him, for he who comes to God must believe that He is, and that He is a rewarder of those who diligently seek Him." Hebrews 11:6

(See also Matthew 6:33.)

THOSE WHO BELIEVE

"'All things are possible to him who believes.'"
—MARK 9:23

1. SHALL RECEIVE REMISSION OF SINS
"'To Him all the prophets witness that, through His name, whoever believes in Him will receive remission of sins.'"
Acts 10:43

(See also Ephesians 1:7; Colossians 1:14.)

2. SHALL NEVER DIE
"And Jesus said to her, 'I am the resurrection and the life. He who believes in Me, though he may die, he shall live. And whoever lives and believes in Me shall never die. Do you believe this?'" John 11:25–26

(See also John 8:51; Revelation 20:6, 14.)

3. SHALL NEVER THIRST
"Jesus said to them, 'I am the bread of life. He who comes to Me shall never hunger, and he who believes in Me shall never thirst.'" John 6:35

4. SHALL BRING FORTH FRUIT
"'He who believes in Me, as the Scripture has said, out of his heart will flow rivers of living water.' But this He spoke concerning the Spirit, whom those who believing in Him would receive; for the Holy Spirit was not yet given, because Jesus was not yet glorified." John 7:38–39

5. SHALL DO GREAT WORKS
"'Most assuredly, I say to you, he who believes in Me, the works that I do he will do also; and greater works than these he will do, because I go to My Father.'" John 14:12

6. SHALL NOT ABIDE IN DARKNESS

"'I have come as a light into the world, that whoever believes in Me should not abide in darkness.'" John 12:46

(See also John 8:12; Colossians 1:13; 1 Peter 2:9.)

7. SHALL BE BORN OF GOD

"Whoever believes that Jesus is the Christ is born of God, and everyone who loves Him who begot also loves him who is begotten of Him." 1 John 5:1

(See also John 1:12–13.)

8. SHALL NOT BE CONDEMNED

"'He who believes in Him is not condemned; but he who does not believe is condemned already, because he has not believed in the name of the only begotten Son of God.'"

John 3:18

(See also John 5:24; Romans 8:1.)

9. SHALL BE COUNTED RIGHTEOUS

"But to him who does not work but believes on Him who justifies the ungodly, his faith is accounted for righteousness."

Romans 4:5

10. SHALL OVERCOME THE WORLD

"For whatever is born of God overcomes the world. And this is the victory that has overcome the world—our faith. Who is he who overcomes the world, but he who believes that Jesus is the Son of God?" 1 John 5:4–5

THE GLORIOUS RESULTS OF FAITH

"So then faith comes by hearing, and hearing by the word of God."

— Romans 10:17 —

1. BY FAITH WE ARE JUSTIFIED

"Therefore, having been justified by faith, we have peace with God through our Lord Jesus Christ." Romans 5:1

2. BY FAITH WE ARE SAVED

"For by grace you have been saved through faith, and that not of yourselves; it is the gift of God, not of works, lest anyone should boast." Ephesians 2:8–9

(See also Acts 16:30–31.)

3. BY FAITH WE ARE SANCTIFIED

"Purifying their hearts by faith." Acts 15:9

"'Who are sanctified by faith in Me.'" Acts 26:18

4. BY FAITH WE RECEIVE THE HOLY SPIRIT

"That the blessing of Abraham might come upon the Gentiles in Christ Jesus, that we might receive the promise of the Spirit through faith." Galatians 3:14

5. BY FAITH WE WALK

"For we walk by faith, not by sight." 2 Corinthians 5:7

(See Also Colossians 2:6.)

6. BY FAITH WE LIVE

"I have been crucified with Christ; it is no longer I who live, but Christ lives in me; and the life which I now live in the flesh I live by faith in the Son of God, who loved me and gave Himself for me." Galatians 2:20

7. BY FAITH WE OVERCOME

"For whatever is born of God overcomes the world. And this
is the victory that has overcome the world—our faith."

1 John 5:4

THE GOSPEL

"For I am not ashamed of the gospel of Christ."

~ Romans 1:16 ~

1. THE CONTENT OF THE GOSPEL

"Moreover, brethren, I declare to you the gospel which I preached to you . . . that Christ died for our sins according to the Scriptures, and that He was buried, and that He rose again the third day according to the Scriptures."

1 Corinthians 15:1, 3–4

(See also John 3:16.)

2. THE TRUTH OF THE GOSPEL

"Because of the hope which is laid up for you in heaven, of which you heard before in the word of the truth of the gospel." Colossians 1:5

3. THE FAITH OF THE GOSPEL

"That you stand fast in one spirit, with one mind striving together for the faith of the gospel." Philippians 1:27

4. THE FURTHERANCE OF THE GOSPEL

"But I want you to know, brethren, that the things which happened to me have actually turned out for the furtherance of the gospel." Philippians 1:12

5. THE AFFLICTIONS OF THE GOSPEL

"But share with me in the sufferings for the gospel according to the power of God." 2 Timothy 1:8

6. THE MYSTERY OF THE GOSPEL

"Praying always . . . that utterance may be given to me, that I may open my mouth boldly to make known the mystery of the gospel." Ephesians 6:18–19

WHY YOU SHOULD BE SAVED

"For all have sinned and fall short of the glory of God."
~ Romans 3:23 ~

1. BECAUSE IT IS GOD'S WILL
"Who desires all men to be saved and to come to the
knowledge of the truth." 1 Timothy 2:4

(See also 2 Peter 3:9.)

2. BECAUSE GOD LOVES YOU
"'For God so loved the world that He gave His only begotten
Son, that whoever believes in Him should not perish but
have everlasting life.'" John 3:16

(See also Romans 5:8; 1 John 4:9.)

3. BECAUSE YOU ARE ALREADY CONDEMNED
"'He who does not believe is condemned already, because he
has not believed in the name of the only begotten Son of
God.'" John 3:18

(See also John 3:36; Romans 3:19.)

4. BECAUSE TOMORROW MAY BE TOO LATE
"Behold, now is the accepted time; behold, now is the day of
salvation." 2 Corinthians 6:2

(See also Proverbs 27:1; Hebrews 3:15.)

5. BECAUSE YOU ARE INVITED TO BE SAVED
"And the Spirit and the bride say, 'Come!' And let him who
hears say, 'Come!' And let him who thirsts come. And
whoever desires, let him take the water of life freely."

Revelation 22:17

(See also Luke 14:17; John 6:37.)

6. BECAUSE YOU WILL HAVE PEACE AND REST

"Therefore, having been justified by faith, we have peace with God through our Lord Jesus Christ." Romans 5:1

(See also John 14:27; Matthew 11:28.)

7. BECAUSE CHRIST JESUS CAME TO SAVE YOU

"This is a faithful saying and worthy of all acceptance, that Christ Jesus came into the world to save sinners, of whom I am chief." 1 Timothy 1:15

(See also Luke 19:10.)

THE GREAT CHRISTMAS MESSAGE

"Then the angel said to them, 'Do not be afraid, for behold, I bring you good tidings of great joy which will be to all people. For there is born to you this day in the city of David a Savior, who is Christ the Lord.'"

— Luke 2:10–11 —

1. THE GREAT PREACHER
"The angel said to them."

2. THE GREAT INTRODUCTION
"'Do not be afraid.'"

3. THE GREAT NEWS
"'Good tidings of great joy.'"

4. THE GREAT HOST
"'Which will be to all people.'"

5. THE GREAT FACT
"'There is born to you . . . a Savior.'"

6. THE GREAT PLACE
"'The city of David.'"

7. THE GREAT SAVIOR
"'Christ the Lord.'"

8. THE GREAT SINNER
"'You.'"

9. THE GREAT MESSAGE FORETOLD
"'Behold, the virgin shall conceive and bear a Son, and shall call His name Immanuel.'" Isaiah 7:14

(See also Isaiah 9:6.)

10. THE GREAT PROMISE GIVEN

"That if you confess with your mouth the Lord Jesus and believe in your heart that God has raised Him from the dead, you will be saved. For with the heart one believes to righteousness, and with the mouth confession is made to salvation." Romans 10:9–10

THE BELIEVER IS JUSTIFIED

"And by Him everyone who believes is justified from all things."
⌐ Acts. 13:39 ¬

1. BY GOD THE FATHER

"Who shall bring a charge against God's elect? It is God who justifies." Romans 8:33

(See Romans 3:26; 4:5.)

2. BY GOD THE SON

"Knowing that a man is not justified by the works of the law but by faith in Jesus Christ, even we have believed in Christ Jesus, that we might be justified by faith in Christ and not by the works of the law; for by the works of the law no flesh shall be justified" Galatians 2:16

(See also 1 Corinthians 6:11.)

3. BY GOD THE HOLY SPIRIT

"Do you not know that the unrighteous will not inherit the kingdom of God? . . . And such were some of you. But you were washed, but you were sanctified, but you were justified in the name of the Lord Jesus and by the Spirit of our God."

1 Corinthians 6:9, 11

4. BY GRACE

"Being justified freely by His grace through the redemption that is in Christ Jesus." Romans 3:24

(See also Titus 3:7.)

5. BY BLOOD

"Much more then, having been justified by His blood, we shall be saved from wrath through Him." Romans 5:9

(See also Romans 3:24–25; Colossians 1:14.)

6. BY FAITH

"Therefore we conclude that a man is justified by faith apart from the deeds of the law." Romans 3:28

(See also Romans 4:5; 5:1; Galatians 3:24.)

7. BY WORKS

"Do you see that faith was working together with his works, and by works faith was made perfect? . . . You see then that a man is justified by works, and not by faith only." James 2:22, 24

COMPLETENESS IN CHRIST

"You are complete in Him."

⌐— Colossians 2:10 —⌐

1. OUR REDEMPTION IS COMPLETE IN CHRIST.
"For what the law could not do in that it was weak through the flesh, God did by sending His own Son in the likeness of sinful flesh, on account of sin: He condemned sin in the flesh." Romans 8:3

2. OUR JUSTIFICATION IS COMPLETE IN CHRIST.
"Therefore, let it be known to you, brethren, that through this Man is preached to you the forgiveness of sins; and by Him everyone who believes is justified from all things from which you could not be justified by the law of Moses." Acts 13:38–39

3. OUR HOLINESS IS COMPLETE IN CHRIST.
"But of Him you are in Christ Jesus, who became for us wisdom from God—and righteousness and sanctification and redemption." 1 Corinthians 1:30

4. OUR PEACE IS COMPLETE IN CHRIST.
"He Himself is our peace." Ephesians 2:14

(See also John 14:27; 16:33.)

5. OUR TRIUMPH IS COMPLETE IN CHRIST.
"Now thanks be to God who always leads us in triumph in Christ." 2 Corinthians 2:14

(See also Romans 8:37; Philippians 4:13.)

6. OUR HAPPINESS AT DEATH IS COMPLETE IN CHRIST.

"Blessed are the dead who die in the Lord from now on. 'Yes,' says the Spirit, 'that they may rest from their labors, and their works follow them.'" Revelation 14:13

(See also Psalm 116:15; Philippians 1:21.)

7. OUR RESURRECTION AND ETERNAL GLORY ARE COMPLETE IN CHRIST.

"Beloved, now we are children of God; and it has not yet been revealed what we shall be, but we know that when He is revealed, we shall be like Him, for we shall see Him as He is."

1 John 3:2

(See also John 11:25–26; Philippians 3:20–21.)

WHOEVER BELIEVES

"And whoever desires, let him take the water of life freely."

— Revelation 22:17 —

1. IS BORN OF GOD

"Whoever believes that Jesus is the Christ is born of God, and everyone who loves Him who begot also loves him who is begotten of Him." 1 John 5:1

2. SHALL HAVE EVERLASTING LIFE

"'For God so loved the world that He gave His only begotten Son, that whoever believes in Him should not perish but have everlasting life.'" John 3:16

3. SHALL RECEIVE REMISSION OF SINS

"'To Him all the prophets witness that, through His name, whoever believes in Him will receive remission of sins.'"

Acts 10:43

4. SHALL NOT ABIDE IN DARKNESS

"'I have come as a light into the world, that whoever believes in Me should not abide in darkness.'" John 12:46

(See also John 8:12.)

5. SHALL NOT BE ASHAMED

"As it is written, 'Behold, I lay in Zion a stumbling stone and rock of offense, and whoever believes on Him will not be put to shame.'" Romans 9:33

(See also 1 Peter 2:6.)

PART FIVE

❧✕☙

HEAVEN AND HELL

1. HEAVEN: ITS NAMES

2. HEAVEN: ITS DESCRIPTION

3. HEAVEN: ITS OCCUPANTS

4. THE HEAVENLY LIFE

5. HELL: ITS DESCRIPTION

6. HELL: ITS OCCUPANTS

HEAVEN: ITS NAMES

"Heaven is My throne, and earth is My footstool."

Isaiah 66:1

1. THE FATHER'S HOUSE

"'In My Father's house are many mansions; if it were not so, I would have told you. I go to prepare a place for you.'" John 14:2

2. THE HOLY PLACE

"For thus says the High and Lofty One who inhabits eternity, whose name is Holy: 'I dwell in the high and holy place, with him who has a contrite and humble spirit.'" Isaiah 57:15

(See also Deuteronomy 26:15; Psalm 20:6.)

3. THE KINGDOM OF CHRIST AND OF GOD

"For this you know, that no fornicator, unclean person, nor covetous man, who is an idolater, has any inheritance in the kingdom of Christ and God." Ephesians 5:5

4. THE HEAVENLY COUNTRY

"But now they desire a better, that is, a heavenly country. Therefore God is not ashamed to be called their God."

Hebrews 11:16

5. THE CITY

"For he waited for the city which has foundations, whose builder and maker is God." Hebrews 11:10

6. PARADISE

"How he was caught up into Paradise and heard inexpressible words, which it is not lawful for a man to utter."

2 Corinthians 12:4

(See also Revelation 2:7.)

7. HOME

"We are confident, yes, well pleased rather to be absent from the body and to be present with the Lord." 2 Corinthians 5:8

HEAVEN: ITS DESCRIPTION

Read Revelation 4, 21–22.

1. HEAVEN IS A PLACE OF REST.
"Then I heard a voice from heaven saying to me, 'Write:
"Blessed are the dead who die in the Lord from now on."'
'Yes,' says the Spirit, 'that they may rest from their labors, and
their works follow them.'" Revelation 14:13

(See also Hebrews 4:9.)

2. HEAVEN IS A PLACE OF LIFE.
"'And God will wipe away every tear from their eyes; there
shall be no more death.'" Revelation 21:4

3. HEAVEN IS A PLACE OF PURITY.
"Now to Him who is able to keep you from stumbling, and to
present you faultless before the presence of His glory with
exceeding joy." Jude 24

(See also Revelation 21:27.)

4. HEAVEN IS A PLACE OF PRAISE AND WORSHIP.
"'Worthy is the Lamb who was slain to receive power and
riches and wisdom and strength and honor and glory and
blessing!'" Revelation 5:12

(See also Revelation 5:8–14.)

5. HEAVEN IS A PLACE OF KNOWLEDGE.
"Now I know in part, but then I shall know just as I also am
known." 1 Corinthians 13:12

6. HEAVEN IS A PLACE OF COMFORT.
"They shall neither hunger anymore nor thirst anymore; the
sun shall not strike them, nor any heat." Revelation 7:16

7. HEAVEN IS A PLACE OF LIGHT AND BEAUTY.

"And the city had no need of the sun or of the moon to shine in it, for the glory of God illuminated it, and the Lamb is its light." Revelation 21:23;

8. HEAVEN IS A PLACE OF REUNION.

"For the Lord Himself will descend from heaven with a shout, with the voice of an archangel, and with the trumpet of God. And the dead in Christ will rise first. Then we who are alive and remain shall be caught up together with them in the clouds to meet the Lord in the air. And thus we shall always be with the Lord." 1 Thessalonians 4:16–17

9. HEAVEN IS A PLACE OF FELLOWSHIP WITH JESUS.

"'I go to prepare a place for you. And if I go and prepare a place for you, I will come again and receive you to Myself; that where I am, there you may be also.'" John 14:2–3

(See also 2 Corinthians 5:8; Philippians 1:23.)

10. HEAVEN IS A PLACE OF SERVICE.

"And there shall be no more curse, but the throne of God and of the Lamb shall be in it, and His servants shall serve Him."

Revelation 22:3

(See also Revelation 7:15.)

11. HEAVEN IS A PLACE LARGELY POPULATED.

"After these things I looked, and behold, a great multitude which no one could number, of all nations, tribes, people, and tongues, standing before the throne and before the Lamb, clothed with white robes, with palm branches in their hands." Revelation 7:9

12. HEAVEN IS A PLACE OF RULERSHIP.

"And there shall be no night there: They need no lamp nor light of the sun, for the Lord God gives them light. And they shall reign forever and ever." Revelation 22:5

(See also Matthew 25:23.)

HEAVEN: ITS OCCUPANTS

" 'I will be their God, and they shall be My people.' "

⌐ Hebrews 8:10 ⌐

1. THEY ARE A REGENERATED PEOPLE.

"Jesus answered and said to him, 'Most assuredly, I say to you, unless one is born again, he cannot see the kingdom of God.' " John 3:3

(See also 2 Corinthians 5:17.)

2. THEY ARE A PERSEVERING PEOPLE.

"But Jesus said to him, 'No one, having put his hand to the plow, and looking back, is fit for the kingdom of God.' "

Luke 9:62

3. THEY ARE A SUFFERING PEOPLE.

"Strengthening the souls of the disciples, exhorting them to continue in the faith, and saying, 'We must through many tribulations enter the kingdom of God.' " Acts 14:22

(See also Matthew 24:13).

4. THEY ARE A HUMBLE PEOPLE.

" 'Blessed are the poor in spirit, for theirs is the kingdom of heaven.' " Matthew 5:3

5. THEY ARE A RIGHTEOUS PEOPLE.

" 'Blessed are the pure in heart, for they shall see God.' "

Matthew 5:8

(See also Romans 3:21–22.)

6. THEY ARE A FAITHFUL PEOPLE.

"But we are not of those who draw back to perdition, but of those who believe to the saving of the soul." Hebrews 10:39

7. THEY ARE AN EXPECTING PEOPLE.

"For our citizenship is in heaven, from which we also eagerly wait for the Savior, the Lord Jesus Christ, who will transform our lowly body that it may be conformed to His glorious body." Philippians 3:20–21

(See also 1 Thessalonians 1:10; Titus 2:12–14.)

THE HEAVENLY LIFE

"Every spiritual blessings in the heavenly places."
— Ephesians 1:3 —

1. LIFE WITHOUT SIN
"Now to Him who is able to keep you from stumbling, and to
present you faultless before the presence of His glory with
exceeding joy." Jude 24

2. LIFE WITHOUT DARKNESS
"And there shall be no night there: They need no lamp nor
light of the sun, for the Lord God gives them light."
Revelation 22:5

3. LIFE WITHOUT DEATH
"'And God will wipe away every tear from their eyes; there
shall be no more death.'" Revelation 21:4

4. LIFE WITHOUT SUFFERING
"'There shall be no more death, nor sorrow, nor crying; and
there shall there be no more pain, for the former things have
passed away.'" Revelation 21:4

5. LIFE WITHOUT CURSE
"And there shall be no more curse, but the throne of God and
of the Lamb shall be in it." Revelation 22:3

6. LIFE WITHOUT SEPARATION
"For the Lord Himself will descend from heaven with a shout,
with the voice of an archangel, and with the trumpet of God.
And the dead in Christ will rise first. Then we who are alive
and remain shall be caught up together with them in the
clouds to meet the Lord in the air. And thus we shall always
be with the Lord." 1 Thessalonians 4:16–17

7. LIFE WITHOUT WEARINESS IN SERVICE

"And there shall be no more curse, but the throne of God and of the Lamb shall be in it, and His servants shall serve Him."

Revelation 22:3

HELL: ITS DESCRIPTION

"'Everlasting fire prepared for the devil and his angels.'"

— Matthew 25:41 —

1. HELL IS A PLACE PREPARED.

"'Then He will also say to those on the left hand, "Depart from Me, you cursed, into the everlasting fire prepared for the devil and his angels.'"* Matthew 25:41

2. HELL IS A PLACE OF LIFE AND CONSCIOUSNESS.

"'Where their worm does not die, and the fire is not quenched.'" Mark 9:44

(See also Luke 16:23.)

3. HELL IS A PLACE OF SORROW AND SUFFERING.

"'The floods of ungodly men made me afraid; the sorrows of Sheol surrounded me.'" 2 Samuel 22:5–6

(See also Psalms 18:5; 116:3; Matthew 13:41–42.)

4. HELL IS A PLACE OF EVERLASTING TORMENT.

"'And the smoke of their torment ascends forever and ever; and they have no rest day or night.'" Revelation 14:11

(See also Daniel 12:2; Luke 16:23; Revelation 20:10.)

5. HELL IS A PLACE OF EVERLASTING PUNISHMENT.

"'And these will go away into everlasting punishment, but the righteous into eternal life.'" Matthew 25:46

(See also 2 Thessalonians 1:9.)

6. HELL IS A PLACE OF EVERLASTING FIRE.

"'And if your foot makes you sin, cut it off. It is better for you to enter life lame, than having two feet, to be cast into hell, into the fire that shall never be quenched.'"

Mark 9:45

(See also Isaiah 33:14; 66:24; Matthew 25:41; Jude 7.)

7. HELL IS A PLACE OF DARKNESS.

"For if God did not spare the angels who sinned, but cast them down to hell and delivered them into chains of darkness, to be reserved for judgment." 2 Peter 2:4

8. HELL IS A PLACE OF EVERLASTING CONTEMPT.

"And many of those who sleep in the dust of the earth shall awake, some to everlasting life, some to shame and everlasting contempt." Daniel 12:2

9. HELL IS A PLACE OF SEPARATION.

"'But Abraham said, "Son, remember that in your lifetime you received your good things, and likewise Lazarus evil things; but now he is comforted and you are tormented. And besides all this, between us and you there is a great gulf fixed, so that those who want to pass from here to you cannot, nor can those from here pass to us".'" Luke 16:25–26

10. HELL WILL HAVE A LARGE POPULATION.

"The wicked shall be turned into hell, and all the nations that forget God." Psalm 9:17

(See also Revelation 21:8.)

HELL: ITS OCCUPANTS

"'Fear Him who is able to destroy both soul and body in hell.'"
— Matthew 10:28 —

1. HELL WILL CONTAIN ALL OF THE WICKED.
"The wicked shall be turned into hell, and all the nations that forget God." Psalm 9:17

(See also Matthew 13:41–42; Revelation 21:8.)

2. HELL WILL CONTAIN ALL WHO KNOW NOT GOD.
"In flaming fire taking vengeance on those who do not know God." 2 Thessalonians 1:8

3. HELL WILL CONTAIN ALL WHO OBEY NOT THE GOSPEL OF CHRIST.
"In flaming fire taking vengeance on . . . those who do not obey the gospel of our Lord Jesus Christ."

2 Thessalonians 1:8

4. HELL WILL CONTAIN ALL WHO WORSHIP THE BEAST.
"Then a third angel followed them, saying with a loud voice, 'If anyone worship the beast and his image, and receives his mark on his forehead or on his hand, he himself shall also drink of the wine of the wrath of God, which is poured out full strength into the cup of His indignation.'" Revelation 14: 9–10

5. HELL WILL CONTAIN ALL WHO ARE NOT WRITTEN IN THE BOOK OF LIFE.
"And anyone not found written in the Book of Life was cast into the lake of fire." Revelation 20:15

6. HELL WILL CONTAIN ALL ANGELS WHO HAVE SINNED.

"For . . . God did not spare the angels who sinned, but cast them down to hell and delivered them into chains of darkness, to be reserved for judgment." 2 Peter 2:4

7. HELL WILL CONTAIN THE DEVIL, BEAST, AND FALSE PROPHET.

"And the devil, who deceived them, was cast into the lake of fire and brimstone where the beast and the false prophet are. And they will be tormented day and night forever and ever."

Revelation 20:10

(See also Revelation 19:20.)

PART SIX

ETERNITY AND THE RESURRECTION

1. WHAT THE BIBLE TEACHES ABOUT
ETERNAL LIFE

2. ETERNAL LIFE

3. ETERNAL REALITIES

4. THE MEANING OF THE EMPTY TOMB

5. THE VALUE OF THE RESURRECTION

WHAT THE BIBLE TEACHES
ABOUT ETERNAL LIFE

"'And I give them eternal life, and they shall never perish; neither shall anyone snatch them out of My hand.'"

— John 10:28 —

1. ETERNAL LIFE IS DESIRED.
"Now behold, one came and said to Him, 'Good Teacher, what good thing shall I do that I may have eternal life?'"

Matthew 19:16

2. ETERNAL LIFE IS PROMISED.
"In hope of eternal life which God, who cannot lie, promised before time began." Titus 1:2

(See also 1 John 2:25.)

3. ETERNAL LIFE IS IN GOD'S SON.
"And we know that the Son of God has come and has given us an understanding, that we may know Him who is true; and we are in Him who is true, in His Son Jesus Christ. This is the true God and eternal life." 1 John 5:20

(See also 1 John 1:1–3.)

4. ETERNAL LIFE IS A GIFT.
"For the wages of sin is death, but the gift of God is eternal life in Christ Jesus our Lord." Romans 6:23

5. ETERNAL LIFE IS RECEIVED BY FAITH.
"But as many as received Him, to them He gave the right to become children of God, even to those who believe in His name." John 1:12

(See also John 3:16; Acts 13:48.)

6. ETERNAL LIFE CAN BE A PRESENT POSSESSION.

"He who has the Son has life; he who does not have the Son of God does not have life." 1 John 5:12

ETERNAL LIFE

"'And this is eternal life, that they may know You.'"

~— John 17:3 —~

1. ETERNAL LIFE WAS WITH THE FATHER.

"The life was manifested, and we have seen and bear witness, and declare to you that eternal life which was with the Father and was manifested to us." 1 John 1:2

(See also John 1:1–2; 17:5.)

2. ETERNAL LIFE WAS MANIFESTED BY CHRIST.

"That which was from the beginning, which we have heard, which we have seen with our eyes, which we have looked upon, and our hands have handled, concerning the Word of life . . . and was manifested to us." 1 John 1:1–2

3. ETERNAL LIFE WAS PROMISED BY THE FATHER.

"And this is the promise that He has promised us— eternal life." 1 John 2:25

(See also Titus 1:2.)

4. ETERNAL LIFE IS NOT POSSESSED BY THE UNRIGHTEOUS.

"Whoever hates his brother is a murderer, and you know that no murderer has eternal life abiding in him." 1 John 3:15

5. ETERNAL LIFE IS GIVING BY THE FATHER.

"And this is the testimony: that God has given us eternal life, and this life is in His Son." 1 John 5:11

"The gift of God is eternal life in Christ Jesus our Lord."

Romans 6:23

6. ETERNAL LIFE IS A PRESENT POSSESSION.

"These things I have written to you who believe in the name of the Son of God, that you may know that you have eternal life." 1 John 5:13

(See also John 3:36; 5:24.)

ETERNAL REALITIES

"The things which are not seen are eternal."

— 2 Corinthians 4:18 —

1. THE ETERNAL GOD

"The eternal God is your refuge, and underneath are the everlasting arms." Deuteronomy 33:27

2. THE ETERNAL KING

"Now to the King eternal, immortal, invisible, to God who alone is wise, be honor and glory forever and ever. Amen." 1 Timothy 1:17

3. THE ETERNAL SPIRIT

"How much more shall the blood of Christ, who through the eternal Spirit offered Himself without spot to God, purge your conscience from dead works to serve the living God?" Hebrews 9:14

4. THE ETERNAL POWER

"For since the creation of the world His invisible attributes are clearly seen, being understood by the things that are made, even His eternal power and Godhead, so that they are without excuse." Romans 1:20

5. THE ETERNAL REDEMPTION

"Not with the blood of goats and calves, but with His own blood He entered the Most Holy Place once for all, having obtained eternal redemption." Hebrews 9:12

6. THE ETERNAL SALVATION

"And having been perfected, He became the author of eternal salvation to all who obey Him." Hebrews 5:9

7. THE ETERNAL LIFE

"For the wages of sin is death, but the gift of God is eternal life in Christ Jesus our Lord." Romans 6:23

"'And these will go away into everlasting punishment, but the righteous into eternal life.'" Matthew 25:46

8. THE ETERNAL HOUSE

"For we know that if our earthly house, this tent, is destroyed, we have a building from God, a house not made with hands, eternal in the heavens." 2 Corinthians 5:1

9. THE ETERNAL INHERITANCE

"And for this reason He is the mediator of the new covenant, by means of death, for the redemption of the transgressions under the first covenant, that those who are called may receive the promise of the eternal inheritance." Hebrews 9:15

(See also 1 Peter 1:4–5.)

10. THE ETERNAL GLORY

"But may the God of all grace, who called us to His eternal glory by Christ Jesus, after you have suffered a while, perfect, establish, strengthen, and settle you." 1 Peter 5:10

(See also 2 Timothy 2:10; 2 Corinthians 4:17.)

11. THE ETERNAL PURPOSE

"To the intent that now the manifold wisdom of God might be made known by the church to the principalities and powers in the heavenly places, according to the eternal purpose which He accomplished in Christ Jesus our Lord."

Ephesians 3:10–11

12. THE ETERNAL FIRE

"As Sodom and Gomorrah, and the cities around them in a similar manner to these, having given themselves over to sexual immorality and gone after strange flesh, are set forth for an example, suffering the vengeance of eternal fire." Jude 7

THE MEANING OF THE EMPTY TOMB

"'Behold My hands and My feet, that it is I Myself'"

⌐ Luke 24:39 ⌐

1. IT MEANS THE FULFILLMENT OF SCRIPTURE.

"For You will not leave my soul in Sheol, nor will You allow Your Holy One to see corruption." Psalm 16:10

2. IT MEANS SALVATION TO ALL WHO BELIEVE.

"That if you confess with your mouth the Lord Jesus and believe in your heart that God has raised Him from the dead, you will be saved. For with the heart one believes to righteousness, and with the mouth confession is made to salvation." Romans 10:9–10

(See also Acts 13:38–39.)

3. IT MEANS JUSTIFICATION TO ALL WHO BELIEVE.

"It shall be imputed to us who believe in Him who raised up Jesus our Lord from the dead, who was delivered up because of our offenses, and was raised because of our justification."

Romans 4:24–25

(See also Romans 5:1.)

4. IT MEANS SANCTIFICATION TO ALL WHO BELIEVE.

"Therefore we were buried with Him through baptism into death, that just as Christ was raised from the dead by the glory of the Father, even so we also should walk in newness of life." Romans 6:4

5. IT MEANS ASSURANCE TO ALL WHO BELIEVE.

"Who through Him believe in God, who raised Him from the dead and gave Him glory, so that your faith and hope are in God." 1 Peter 1:21

6. IT MEANS VICTORY TO ALL WHO BELIEVE.

"But now Christ is risen from the dead, and has become the firstfruits of those who have fallen asleep. . . But each one in his own order: Christ the firstfruits, afterward those who are Christ's at His coming. . . . But thanks be to God, who gives us the victory through our Lord Jesus Christ."

1 Corinthians 15:20, 23, 57

7. IT MEANS A RIGHTEOUS JUDGMENT.

"'Because He has appointed a day on which He will judge the world in righteousness by the Man whom He has ordained. He has given assurance of this to all by raising Him from the dead.'" Acts 17:31

8. IT MEANS REUNION WITH DEPARTED ONES.

"For the Lord Himself will descend from heaven with a shout, with the voice of an archangel, and with the trumpet of God. And the dead in Christ will rise first. Then we who are alive and remain shall be caught up together with them in the clouds to meet the Lord in the air. And thus we shall always be with the Lord." 1 Thessalonians 4:16–17

9. IT MEANS FELLOWSHIP WITH JESUS IN GLORY.

"Knowing that He who raised up the Lord Jesus will also raise us up with Jesus, and will present us with you."

2 Corinthians 4:14

(See also 1 Corinthians 6:14.)

10. IT MEANS A RICH INHERITANCE.

"Blessed be the God and Father of our Lord Jesus Christ, who according to His abundant mercy has begotten us again to a living hope through the resurrection of Jesus Christ from the dead, to an inheritance incorruptible and undefiled and that does not fade away, reserved in heaven for you." 1 Peter 1:3–4

THE VALUE OF THE RESURRECTION

"And if Christ is not risen, your faith is futile."
⌒ 1 Corinthians 15:17 ⌒

1. NECESSARY TO OUR SALVATION
"That if you confess with your mouth the Lord Jesus and believe in your heart that God has raised Him from the dead,
you will be saved." Romans 10:9

2. INSURES OUR JUSTIFICATION
"Who was delivered up because of our offenses, and was
raised because of our justification." Romans 4:25

3. GIVES US SECURITY
"Therefore He is also able to save to the uttermost those who
come to God through Him, since He ever lives to make
intercession for them." Hebrews 7:25

4. PRODUCES FRUITFULNESS
"Therefore, my brethren, you also have become dead to the
law through the body of Christ, that you may be married to
another, even to Him who was raised from the dead, that we
should bear fruit to God." Romans 7:4

5. ENERGIZES BELIEVERS
"For if when we were enemies we were reconciled to God
through the death of His Son, much more, having been
reconciled, we shall be saved by His life." Romans 5:10
(See also Galatians 2:20.)

6. ASSURES OF RIGHTEOUS JUDGMENT
"'Because He has appointed a day on which He will judge the
world in righteousness by the Man whom He has
ordained. He has given assurance of this to all by raising
Him from the dead.'" Acts 17:31

7. GUARANTEES OUR RESURRECTION

"'Because I live, you will live also.'" John 14:19

(See also 1 Corinthians 15:20–23; 1 Thessalonians 4:13–18.)

PART SEVEN

JESUS

1. THE BIRTH OF CHRIST

2. JESUS

3. THE DEITY OF CHRIST

4. WITNESSES TO CHRIST'S DEITY

5. THE UNSPEAKABLE GIFT

6. OUR WONDERFUL SAVIOR

7. THE "I WILLS" OF CHRIST

8. THE BLOOD OF CHRIST

9. WHAT GOD HAS GIVEN CHRIST

10. THE GLORIOUS POWER OF CHRIST

THE BIRTH OF CHRIST

"Christ Jesus came into the world to save sinners."
⌐ 1 Timothy 1:15 ¬

1. PREDESTINED BEFORE THE WORLD BEGAN
"He indeed was foreordained before the foundation of the world, but was manifest in these last times for you."

1 Peter 1:20

(See also Ephesians 1:4–5.)

2. PROMISED BY THE FATHER
"'And I will put enmity between you and the woman, and between your seed and her Seed; He shall bruise your head, and you shall bruise His heel.'" Genesis 3:15

3. PROPHESIED BY THE PROPHETS
"Therefore the Lord Himself will give you a sign: 'Behold, the virgin shall conceive and bear a son, and shall call His name Immanuel.'" Isaiah 7:14

(See also Isaiah 9:6; Micah 5:2.)

4. PROVIDENTIALLY EFFECTED
"And it came to pass in those days that a decree went out from Caesar Augustus that all the world should be registered. . . . And Joseph also went up from Galilee . . . to be registered with Mary, his betrothed wife, who was with child." Luke 2:1, 4–5

5. PRESENTED IN THE FULLNESS OF TIME
"But when the fullness of time had come, God sent forth His Son, born of a woman, born under the law, to redeem those who were under the law, that we might receive the adoption as sons." Galatians 4:4–5

6. PROCLAIMED BY THE ANGEL

"Then the angel said to them, 'Do not be afraid, for behold, I bring you good tidings of great joy which will be to all people. For there is born to you this day in the city of David a Savior, who is Christ the Lord.'" Luke 2:10–11

7. PREPARATORY FOR SALVATION

"'And she will bring forth a Son, and you shall call His name Jesus, for He will save His people from their sins.'"

Matthew 1:21

(See also John 1:10–14; 3:16.)

JESUS

"'And you shall call His name JESUS, for He will save His people from their sins.'"

^— Matthew 1:21 —^

1. THE FATHER OF JESUS
"Therefore the Jews sought all the more to kill Him, because He not only broke the Sabbath, but also said that God was His Father, making Himself equal with God." John 5:18

2. THE MOTHER OF JESUS
"Now there stood by the cross of Jesus His mother. . . . When Jesus therefore saw His mother, and the disciple whom He loved standing by, He said to His mother, 'Woman, behold your son!'" John 19:25–26

(See also John 2:3; Acts 1:14.)

3. THE BIRTH OF JESUS
"Now the birth of Jesus Christ was as follows: After His mother Mary was bethrothed to Joseph, before they came together, she was found with child of the Holy Spirit."

Matthew 1:18

4. THE LIFE OF JESUS
"Who is holy, harmless, undefiled, separate from sinners."

Hebrews 7:26

(See also Hebrews 4:15.)

5. THE CROSS OF JESUS
"But God forbid that I should glory except in the cross of our Lord Jesus Christ, by whom the world has been crucified to me, and I to the world." Galatians 6:14

6. THE BLOOD OF JESUS

"Elect according to the foreknowledge of God the Father, in sanctification of the Spirit, for obedience and sprinkling of the blood of Jesus Christ." 1 Peter 1:2

(See also 1 Peter 1:19; Hebrews 10:19.)

7. THE DYING OF JESUS

"Always carrying about in the body the dying of the Lord Jesus, that the life of Jesus also may be manifested in our body." 2 Corinthians 4:10

8. THE BODY OF JESUS

"After this, Joseph of Arimathea, being a disciple of Jesus, but secretly, for fear of the Jews, asked Pilate that he might take away the body of Jesus; and Pilate gave him permission. So he came and took the body of Jesus." John 19:38

(See also John 19:40; 20:12; Hebrews 10:10.)

9. THE RESURRECTION OF JESUS

"Blessed be the God and Father of our Lord Jesus Christ, who according to His abundant mercy has begotten us again to a living hope through the resurrection of Jesus Christ from the dead." 1 Peter 1:3

(See also Acts 4:33.)

10. THE POWER OF JESUS

"And declared to be the Son of God with power, according to the Spirit of holiness, by the resurrection from the dead."

Romans 1:4

(See also Matthew 28:18; John 17:2; 1 Corinthians 1:24.)

11. THE GRACE OF JESUS

"'But we believe that through the grace of the Lord Jesus Christ we shall be saved in the same manner as they.'"

Acts 15:11

(See also 2 Corinthians 8:9.)

THE DEITY OF CHRIST

"Jesus said to them . . . 'Before Abraham was, I am.'"
∽ John 8:58 ∽

1. PROCLAIMED BY THE FATHER

"While he was still speaking, behold, a bright cloud overshadowed them; and suddenly a voice came out of the cloud, saying, 'This is My beloved Son, in whom I am well pleased! Hear Him!'" Matthew 17:5

(See also Matthew 3:16–17.)

2. CLAIMED BY THE SON

"Jesus said to him, 'Have I been with you so long, and yet you have not known Me, Philip? He who has seen Me has seen the Father; so how can you say, 'Show us the Father?'" John 14:9

(See also John 10:30–33; 17:5.)

3. WITNESSED BY THE SPIRIT

"And immediately, coming up from the water, He saw the heavens parting and the Spirit descending upon Him like a dove." Mark 1:10

4. ACKNOWLEDGED BY ANGELS

"Then the angel said to them, 'Do not be afraid, for behold, I bring you good tidings of great joy which will be to all people. For there is born to you this day in the city of David a Savior, who is Christ the Lord." Luke 2:10–11

5. CONFESSED BY SAINTS

"And Thomas answered and said to Him, 'My Lord and my God!'" John 20:28

(See also 1 John 1:1–3.)

6. FEARED BY DEMONS

"When He had come to the other side, to the country of the
Gergesenes, there met Him two demon-possessed men,
coming out of the tombs, exceedingly fierce, so that no one
could pass by that way. And suddenly they cried out, saying,
'What have we to do with You, Jesus, You Son of God? Have
You come here to torment us before the time?'" Matthew 8:28–29

(See also Mark 5:7; Luke 4:41; James 2:19.)

7. MANIFESTED BY HIS WORKS

"'But I have a greater witness than John's; for the works which
the Father has given Me to finish—the very works that I
do—bear witness of Me, that the Father has sent Me.'"

John 5:36

(See also John 14:10–11; Colossians 1:16).

WITNESSES TO CHRIST'S DEITY

"'You, being a Man, make Yourself God.'"

~— John 10:33 —~

1. JOHN THE BAPTIST

"'And I have seen and testified that this is the Son of God.'"

John 1:34

(See also John 5:33–36.)

2. JOHN THE APOSTLE

"And we beheld His glory, the glory as of the only begotten of the father, full of grace and truth." John 1:14

(See also 1 John 1:1–4.)

3. PAUL THE APOSTLE

"Then Paul, as his custom was, went in to them, and for three Sabbaths reasoned with them from the Scriptures, explaining and demonstrating that the Christ had to suffer and rise again from the dead, and saying, 'This Jesus whom I preach to you, is the Christ.'" Acts 17:2–3

(See also Philippians 2:6; Colossians 1:15; 1 Timothy 1:17.)

4. A CENTURION

"Now when the centurion and those with him, who were guarding Jesus, saw the earthquake and the things that had happened, they feared greatly, saying, 'Truly this was the Son of God.'" Matthew 27:54

5. STEPHEN

"But he, being full of the Holy Spirit, gazed into heaven, and saw the glory of God, and Jesus standing at the right hand of God, and said, 'Look! I see the heavens opened and the Son of Man standing at the right hand of God!'" Acts 7:55–56

6. NATHANAEL

"Nathanael answered and said to Him, 'Rabbi, You are the Son of God! You are the King of Israel!'" John 1:49

7. MARTHA

"She said to Him, 'Yes, Lord, I believe that You are the Christ, the Son of God, who is to come into the world.'" John 11:27

8. THOMAS

"And Thomas answered and said to Him, 'My Lord and my God!'" John 20:28

THE UNSPEAKABLE GIFT

"Thanks be to God for His indescribable gift!"
^— 2 Corinthians 9:15 —^

1. A PROPHESIED GIFT

"And I will put enmity between you and the woman, and between your seed and her Seed; He shall bruise your head, and you shall bruise His heel." Genesis 3:15

(See also Isaiah 7:14; 9:6.)

2. A SACRIFICIAL GIFT

"For indeed Christ, our Passover, was sacrificed for us."

1 Corinthians 5:7

3. A NECESSARY GIFT

"Jesus said to him, 'I am the way, the truth, and the life. No one comes to the Father except through Me.'" John 14:6

(See also 1 John 2:23; 5:12.)

4. A SUFFICIENT GIFT

"And you are complete in Him." Colossians 2:10
"Christ is all and in all." Colossians 3:11

5. A PRECIOUS GIFT

"Therefore, to you who believe, He is precious." 1 Peter 2:7

6. A FREE GIFT

"Therefore, as through one man's offense judgment came to all men, resulting in condemnation, even so through one Man's righteous act the free gift came to all men, resulting in justification of life." Romans 5:18

7. A UNIVERSAL GIFT
"'For God so loved the world that He gave His only begotten Son.'" John 3:16

8. AN INDIVIDUAL GIFT
"'For God so loved the world that He gave His only begotten Son, that whoever believes in Him should not perish but have everlasting life.'" John 3:16

9. A PRESENT GIFT
"Behold, now is the accepted time; behold, now is the day of salvation." 2 Corinthians 6:2

(See also Hebrews 3:15.)

10. AN ETERNAL GIFT
"'And this is eternal life, that they may know You' the only true God, and Jesus Christ whom You have sent.'" John 17:3
"Jesus Christ is the same yesterday, today, and forever."

Hebrews 13:8

11. AN ACCEPTED GIFT . . . A REJECTED GIFT
"'But as many as received Him, to them He gave the right to become children of God, even to those who believe in His name.'" John 1:12
"'But you are not willing to come to Me that you may have life.'" John 5:40

12. AN UNAPPRECIATED GIFT
"Jesus answered and said to her, 'If you knew the gift of God, and who it is who says to you, "Give me to drink," you would have asked Him, and He would have given you living water.'"

John 4:10

(See also Matthew 23:37; Luke 19:41–42.)

OUR WONDERFUL SAVIOR

"His name will be called Wonderful."

Isaiah 9:6

W — WONDERFUL IN HIS WORK

"Jesus answered and said to them, 'I did one work, and you all marvel.'" John 7:21

(See also John 9:4; 17:4.)

O — WONDERFUL IN HIS OFFERING

"By that will we have been sanctified through the offering of the body of Jesus Christ once for all." Hebrews 10:10

(See also Hebrews 10: 14,18.)

N — WONDERFUL IN HIS NATURE

"For in Him dwells all the fullness of the Godhead bodily."

Colossians 2:9

(See also John 10:30; 14:9.)

D — WONDERFUL IN HIS DEEDS

"'Most assuredly, I say to you, the Son can do nothing of Himself, but what He sees the Father do; for whatever He does, the Son also does in like manner.'" John 5:19

(See also Mark 7:37.)

E — WONDERFUL IN HIS EXAMPLE

"For to this you were called, because Christ also suffered for us, leaving us an example, that you should follow His steps."

1 Peter 2:21

R — WONDERFUL IN HIS REDEMPTION

"In whom we have redemption through His blood, the forgiveness of sins." Colossians 1:14

(See also Ephesians 1:7; 1 Peter 1:18–20.)

F — WONDERFUL IN HIS FORBEARANCE

"And the chief priests accused Him of many things, but He answered nothing. Then Pilate asked Him again, saying, 'Do You answer nothing? See how many things they testify against You!' But Jesus still said nothing, so that Pilate marveled." Mark 15:3–5

U — WONDERFUL IN HIS UNION

"'That they all may be one, as You, Father, are in Me, and I in You; that they also may be one in Us, that the world may believe that You sent Me.'" John 17:21

L — WONDERFUL IN HIS LOVE

"'Greater love has no one than this, than to lay down one's life for his friends.'" John 15:13

(See also John 13:1.)

THE "I WILLS" OF CHRIST

"'I will not leave you as orphans; I will come to you.'"
~ John 14:18 ~

1. I WILL GIVE MY FLESH.

"'I am the living bread which came down from heaven. If anyone eats of this bread, he will live forever; and the bread that I shall give is My flesh, which I shall give for the life of the world.'" John 6:51

(See also John 10:11, 17–18.)

2. I WILL GIVE YOU REST.

"'Come to Me, all you who labor and are heavy laden, and I will give you rest.'" Matthew 11:28

3. I WILL GIVE YOU WISDOM.

"'For I will give you a mouth and wisdom which all your adversaries will not be able to contradict or resist.'" Luke 21:15

4. I WILL CONFESS YOU BEFORE MY FATHER.

"'Therefore whoever confesses Me before men, him I will also confess before My Father who is in heaven. But whoever denies Me before men, him I will also deny before my Father who is in heaven.'" Matthew 10:32–33

5. I WILL PRAY.

"'And I will pray the Father, and He will give you another Helper, that He may abide with you forever.'" John 14:16

6. I WILL MAKE.

"'And He said to them, 'Follow Me, and I will make you fishers of men.'" Matthew 4:19
"'You were faithful over a few things, I will make you ruler over many things.'" Matthew 25:21

7. I WILL DO.

"'And whatever you shall ask in My name, that I will do, that the Father may be glorified in the Son. If you ask anything in My name, I will do it." John 14:13–14

8. I WILL DRAW.

"'And I, if I am lifted up from the earth, will draw all peoples to Myself.' This He said, signifying by what death He would die." John 12:32–33

9. I WILL NEVER LEAVE YOU.

"'Let your conduct be without covetousness, and be content with such things as you have. For He Himself has said, 'I will never leave you, nor forsake you.'" Hebrews 13:5
"'I will not leave you orphans; I will come to you.'" John 14:18

10. I WILL BY NO MEANS CAST OUT.

"'All that the Father gives Me will come to Me, and the one who comes to Me I will by no means cast out.'" John 6:37

11. I WILL RAISE YOU UP.

"'Whoever eats My flesh and drinks My blood has eternal life, and I will raise him up at the last day.'" John 6:54

(See also John 6: 39–40, 44; 1 Corinthians 6:14.)

12. I WILL COME AGAIN.

"'And if I go and prepare a place for you, I will come again and receive you to Myself; that where I am, there you may be also.'" John 14:3

(See also Acts 1:10–11.)

THE BLOOD OF CHRIST

"'The church of God which He purchased with His own blood.'"
~ Acts 20:28 ~

SEVEN THINGS OBTAINED
BY THE BLOOD OF CHRIST:

1. REDEMPTION
"He has delivered us from the power of darkness and translated us into the kingdom of the Son of His love, in whom we have redemption through His blood, the forgiveness of sins." Colossians 1:13–14

(See also Ephesians 1:7; 1 Peter 1:18, 19.)

2. JUSTIFICATION
"Much more then, having now been justified by His blood, we shall be saved from wrath through Him." Romans 5:9

(See also Romans 3:24; 4:25.)

3. FORGIVENESS
"In Him we have . . . the forgiveness of sins, according to the riches of His grace." Ephesians 1:7

4. SANCTIFICATION
"Therefore Jesus also, that He might sanctify the people with His own blood, suffered outside the gate." Hebrews 13:12

(See also Hebrews 10:10–14.)

5. PEACE
"For it pleased the Father that in Him all the fullness should dwell, . . . having made peace through the blood of His cross." Colossians 1:19–20

(See also Romans 5:1.)

6. ACCESS

"Therefore, brethren, having boldness to enter the Holiest
by the blood of Jesus, by a new and living way which He
consecrated for us, through the veil, that is, His flesh."

Hebrews 10:19–20

(See also Ephesians 2:13.)

7. VICTORY

"And they overcame him [Satan] by the blood of the Lamb
and by the word of their testimony, and they did not love
their lives to the death." Revelation 12:11

WHAT GOD HAS GIVEN CHRIST

"All things were created through Him and for Him."

⌒ Colossians 1:16 ⌒

1. ALL THINGS INTO HIS HAND

"'The Father loves the Son, and has given all things into His hand.'" John 3:35

(See also Colossians 1:16–18.)

2. LIFE IN HIMSELF

"'For as the Father has life in Himself, so He has granted the Son to have life in Himself.'" John 5:26

(See also John 1:4; 10:10.)

3. ALL AUTHORITY

"'All authority has been given to Me in heaven and on earth.'"

Matthew 28:18

(See also John 17:2.)

4. AUTHORITY TO JUDGE

"'And has given Him authority to execute judgment also, because He is the Son of Man.'" John 5:27

(See also John 5:30; 8:16, 26; 2 Timothy 4:1.)

5. A CUP TO DRINK

"Then Jesus said to Peter, 'Put your sword into the sheath. Shall I not drink the cup which My Father has given Me?'"

John 18:11

6. SOULS AND GLORY

"'Father, I desire that they also whom You gave Me may be with Me where I am, that they may behold My glory which You have given Me; for You loved Me before the foundation of the world.'" John 17:24

(See also John 17: 6, 9, 11; 6:39.)

7. RIGHT TO REIGN

"For He must reign till He has put all enemies under his feet. The last enemy that will be destroyed is death. For 'He has put all things under His feet.' . . . Now when all things are made subject to Him, then the Son Himself will also be subject to Him who put all things under him, that God may be all in all.'" 1 Corinthians 15:25–28

THE GLORIOUS POWER OF CHRIST

"'As You have given [the Son] authority over all flesh.'"
— John 17:2 —

1. IN CREATING

"For by Him all things were created that are in heaven and that are on earth, visible and invisible, whether thrones or dominions or principalities or powers. All things were created through Him and for Him." Colossians 1:16

(See also John 1:1–3.)

2. IN SAVING

"This is a faithful saying and worthy of all acceptance, that Christ Jesus came into the world to save sinners."

1 Timothy 1:15

(See also Luke 19:10; Galatians 1:4; 2 Corinthians 1:10.)

3. IN FORGIVING

"When Jesus saw their faith, He said to the paralytic, 'Son, your sins are forgiven you. . . . But that you may know that the Son of Man has power on earth to forgive sins . . . I say to you, arise.'" Mark 2:5, 10–11

4. IN SANCTIFYING

"By that will we have been sanctified through the offering of the body of Jesus Christ once for all." Hebrews 10:10

(See also Hebrews 10:14; 1 Corinthians 6:11.)

5 IN HEALING

"Then Jesus put out His hand and touched him, saying, 'I am willing; be cleansed.' And immediately his leprosy was cleansed." Matthew 8:3

(See also Matthew 8: 7, 15; Exodus 15:26.)

6. IN STRENGTHENING

"Strengthened with all might, according to His glorious power." Colossians 1:11

(See also Philippians 4:13.)

7. IN PROTECTING

"Who are kept by the power of God through faith for salvation ready to be revealed in the last time." 1 Peter 1:5

(See also Jude 24.)

PART EIGHT

PICTURES OF JESUS

1. THE HANDS OF JESUS

2. THE TOUCH OF JESUS

3. THE FACE OF JESUS

4. THE LOOKS OF JESUS

5. THE CRIES OF JESUS

6. THE GOOD SHEPHERD AND HIS SHEEP

7. MY SHEPHERD

8. WHO CHRIST IS TO BELIEVERS

THE HANDS OF JESUS

"I muse on the work of Your hands."

— Psalm 143:5 —

1. CREATING HANDS

"'Heaven is My throne, and earth is My footstool. What house will you build for Me? says the Lord, or what is the place of My rest? Has My hand not made all these things?'"

Acts 7:49–50

(See also John 1:3; Hebrews 1:2, 10.)

2. SAVING HANDS

"But when he saw the wind was boisterous, he was afraid; and beginning to sink he cried out, saying, 'Lord, save me!' And immediately Jesus stretched out His hand and caught him, and said to him, 'O you of little faith, why did you doubt?'"

Matthew 14:30–31

3. DELIVERING HANDS

"'Woman, you are loosed from your infirmity.' And He laid His hands on her, and immediately she was made straight, and glorified God. . . . 'So ought not this woman, being a daughter of Abraham, whom Satan has bound—think of it— for eighteen years, be loosed from this bond on the Sabbath?'" Luke 13:12–13, 16

4. CLEANSING HANDS

"And behold, a leper came and worshiped Him, saying, 'Lord, if You are willing, You can make me clean.' Then Jesus put out His hand and touched him, saying, 'I am willing; be cleansed.' And immediately his leprosy was cleansed." Matthew 8:2–3

5. LIFE-GIVING HANDS

"'My daughter has just died, but come and lay Your hand upon her and she will live.' . . . But when the crowd was put outside, He went in and took her by the hand, and the girl arose." Matthew 9:18, 25

6. HEALING HANDS

"Now when the sun was setting, all those who had anyone sick with various diseases brought them to Him; and He laid His hands on every one of them and healed them." Luke 4:40

(See also Mark 6:5.)

7. COMFORTING HANDS

"'Assuredly, I say to you, whoever does not receive the kingdom of God as a little child will by no means enter it.' And He took them up in His arms, put His hands on them, and blessed them." Mark 10:15–16

(See also Luke 24:50; Revelation 1:17.)

8. PROTECTING HANDS

"'My sheep hear My voice, and I know them, and they follow Me. And I give them eternal life, and they shall never perish; neither shall anyone snatch them out of My hand.'"

John 10:27–28

(See also Deuteronomy 33:3.)

9. WOUNDED HANDS

"'Unless I see in His hands the print of the nails, and put my finger into the print of the nails, and put my hand into His side, I will not believe.'" John 20:25

(See also John 20:27–28.)

10. RESURRECTED HANDS

"'Behold My hands and My feet, that it is I Myself. Handle Me and see, for a spirit does not have flesh and bones as you see I have.' When He had said this He showed them His hands and His feet." Luke 24:39–40

THE TOUCH OF JESUS

"Suddenly, a hand touched me."

~ Daniel 10:10 ~

1. LIFE-GIVING TOUCH

"Then He came and touched the open coffin, and those who carried him stood still. And he said, 'Young man, I say to you, arise.' And he who was dead sat up and began to speak."

Luke 7:14–15

2. CLEANSING TOUCH

"Then Jesus put out His hand, and touched him, saying, 'I am willing; be cleansed.' And immediately his leprosy was cleansed." Matthew 8:3

3. COOLING TOUCH

"And He touched her hand and the fever left her. Then she arose and served them." Matthew 8:15

4. HEALING TOUCH

"Then He touched their eyes, saying, 'According to your faith let it be to you.' And their eyes were opened."

Matthew 9:29–30

(See also Luke 22:51.)

5. CONSOLING TOUCH

"But Jesus came and touched them and said, 'Arise, and do not be afraid.'" Matthew 17:7

6. COMPASSIONATE TOUCH

"So Jesus had compassion and touched their eyes. And immediately their eyes received sight, and they followed Him." Matthew 20:34

7. MERCIFUL TOUCH

"And He took him aside from the multitude, and put His fingers in his ears, and He spat and touched his tongue. Then, looking up to heaven, He sighed, . . . Immediately his ears were opened, and the impediment of his tongue was loosed, and he spoke plainly." Mark 7:33–35

THE FACE OF JESUS

"For it is the God who commanded light to shine out of darkness who has shone in our hearts to give the light of the knowledge of the glory of God in the face of Jesus Christ."

— 2 Corinthians 4:6 —

1. A SHINING FACE

"His face shone like the sun, and His clothes became as white as the light." Matthew 17:2

(See also Revelation 1:14.)

2. A DETERMINED FACE

"Now it came to pass, when the time had come for Him to be received up, that He steadfastly set His face to go to Jerusalem." Luke 9:51

(See also Isaiah 50:7.)

3. A BRUISED FACE

"Now the men who held Jesus mocked Him and beat Him. And having blindfolded Him, they struck Him on the face and asked Him, saying, 'Prophesy! Who is it that struck You?'" Luke 22:63–64

(See also Isaiah 50:6.)

4. A HATED FACE

"Then they spat in His face and beat Him; and others struck Him with the palms of their hands." Matthew 26:67

5. A HIDDEN FACE: WHY?

"You have hidden Your face from us . . . because of our iniquities." Isaiah 64:7

(See also Deuteronomy 31:17–18; 32:20; Job 13:23–24; Ezekiel 39:24; Micah 3:4.)

6. A FACE AGAINST THEM THAT DO EVIL

"'The face of the Lord is against those who do evil.'" 1 Peter 3:12

(See also Ezekiel 14:8; 15:7; Jeremiah 44:10–11.)

7. A FACE WE SHOULD SEEK

"When You said, 'Seek My face,' my heart said to You, 'Your face, Lord, I will seek.'" Psalm 27:8

(See also 1 Chronicles 16:11; 2 Chronicles 7:14; Psalm 105:4; Hosea 5:15.)

THE LOOKS OF JESUS

"The eyes of the Lord are in every place, keeping watch on the evil and the good."

— Proverbs 15:3 —

1. A LOOK OF DISPLEASURE

"So when He had looked around at them with anger, being grieved for the hardness of their hearts, He said to the man, 'Stretch out your hand.' And he stretched it out, and his hand was restored as whole as the other." Mark 3:5

2. A LOOK OF RECOGNITION

"And He looked around in a circle at those who sat about Him, and said, 'Here are My mother and My brothers! For whoever does the will of God is My brother and My sister, and mother.'" Mark 3:34–35

3. A LOOK OF PLEASURE

"And He looked around to see her who had done this thing. And He said to her, 'Daughter, your faith has made you well.'" Mark 5:32, 34

4. A LOOK OF PRAYER

"And when He had taken the five loaves and the two fish, He looked up to heaven, blessed and broke the loaves, and gave them to His disciples to set before them; and the two fish He divided among them all." Mark 6:41

5. A LOOK OF REPROOF

"But when He had turned around and looked at His disciples, He rebuked Peter, saying, 'Get behind Me, Satan! For you are not mindful of the things of God, but the things of men.'"

Mark 8:33

6. A LOOK OF WARNING

"Then Jesus looked around and said to His disciples, 'How hard it is for those who have riches to enter the kingdom of God!'" Mark 10:23

7. A LOOK OF INSPECTION

"Now Jesus sat opposite the treasury and saw how the people put money into the treasury. And many who were rich put in much." Mark 12:41

THE CRIES OF JESUS

"A man of sorrows and acquainted with grief."
Isaiah 53:3

1. THE CRY OF THE PREACHER
"When He had said these things He cried, 'He who has ears to hear, let him hear!'" Luke 8:8

2. THE CRY OF THE TEACHER
"Then Jesus cried out, as He taught in the temple, saying, 'You both know Me, and you know where I am from; and I have not come of Myself, but He who sent Me is true, whom you do not know.'" John 7:28

3. THE CRY OF THE BENEFACTOR
"On the last day, that great day of the feast, Jesus stood and cried out, saying, 'If anyone thirsts, let him come unto Me and drink. He who believes in Me, as the Scripture has said, out of his heart will flow rivers of living water.'" John 7:37–38

4. THE CRY OF THE LIFE-GIVER
"Now when He had said these things, He cried with a loud voice, 'Lazarus, come forth!'" John 11:43

(See also John 5:28–29.)

5. THE CRY OF THE LIGHT-GIVER
"Then Jesus cried out and said, 'He who believes in Me, believes not in Me but in Him who sent Me. And he who sees Me sees Him who sent Me. I have come as a light into the world, that whoever believes in Me should not abide in darkness.'" John 12:44–46

6. THE CRY OF THE SUFFERER

"And about the ninth hour Jesus cried out with a loud voice, saying, 'Eli, Eli, lama sabachthani?' that is, 'My God, My God, why have You forsaken Me?'" Matthew 27:46

7. THE CRY OF THE SAVIOR

"And when Jesus had out cried with a loud voice, He said, 'Father, into Your hands I commend My spirit.' And having said this, He breathed His last." Luke 23:46

8. THE WORDS OF THE VICTOR

"Then Jesus came and spoke to them, saying, 'All authority has been given to Me in heaven and on earth.'" Matthew 28:18

THE GOOD SHEPHERD AND HIS SHEEP

"I am the good shepherd."

— John 10:11 (and 14) —

1. THE GOOD SHEPHERD CALLS HIS SHEEP.

"'He calls his own sheep by name.'" John 10:3

"'The sheep hear his voice.'" John 10:3

2. THE GOOD SHEPHERD LEADS HIS SHEEP.

"'He . . . leads them out. . . . and the sheep follow him.'"

John 10:3–4

3. THE GOOD SHEPHERD FEEDS HIS SHEEP.

"'Will go in and out and find pasture.'" John 10:9

4. THE GOOD SHEPHERD CARES FOR HIS SHEEP.

"'I have come that they may have life, and that they may have it more abundantly.'" John 10:10

(See John 10:9.)

5. THE GOOD SHEPHERD KNOWS HIS SHEEP.

"'I am the good shepherd; and I know My sheep.'" John 10:14

6. THE GOOD SHEPHERD PROTECTS HIS SHEEP.

"'And I give them eternal life, and they shall never perish; neither shall anyone snatch them out of My hand.'" John 10:28

7. THE GOOD SHEPHERD DIES FOR HIS SHEEP.

"'I am the good shepherd. The good shepherd gives His life for the sheep.'" John 10:11

MY SHEPHERD

"The Lord is my shepherd."

Psalm 23:1

1. THE COMPASSIONATE SHEPHERD
"And Jesus, when He came out, saw a great multitude and was moved with compassion for them, because they were like sheep not having a shepherd. So He began to teach them many things." Mark 6:34

2. THE SMITTEN SHEPHERD
"Then Jesus said to them, 'All of you will be made to stumble because of Me this night, for it is written: "I will strike the Shepherd, and the sheep will be scattered."'" Mark 14:27

(See also Isaiah 53:4; Zechariah 13:7.)

3. THE GOOD SHEPHERD
"'I am the good shepherd. The good shepherd gives His life for the sheep.'" John 10:11

4. THE SEEKING SHEPHERD
"'What man of you, having a hundred sheep, if he loses one of them, does not leave the ninety-nine in the wilderness, and go after the one which is lost until he finds it?'" Luke 15:4

5. THE REJOICING SHEPHERD
"'And when he has found it, he lays it on his shoulders, rejoicing.'" Luke 15:5

6. THE GREAT SHEPHERD
"Now may the God of peace who brought up our Lord Jesus from the dead , that great Shepherd of the sheep, through the blood of the everlasting covenant, make you complete in every good work to do His will." Hebrews 13:20–21

7. THE CHIEF SHEPHERD

"And when the Chief Shepherd appears, you will receive the crown of glory that does not fade away." 1 Peter 5:4

WHO CHRIST IS TO BELIEVERS

"Jesus Christ is the same yesterday, today, and forever."

~ Hebrews13:8 ~

1. OUR PASSOVER

"For indeed Christ, our Passover, was sacrificed for us."

1 Corinthians 5:7

2. OUR SAVIOR

"Looking for the blessed hope and glorious appearing of our great God and Savior Jesus Christ." Titus 2:13

(See also Luke 2:27-30; 2 Timothy 1:10; Titus 1:4; 3:6.)

3. OUR RIGHTEOUSNESS

"Now this is His name by which He will be called: The Lord Our Righteousness." Jeremiah 23:6

(See also Romans 3:21–26; 1 Corinthians 1:30.)

4. OUR PEACE

"For He Himself is our peace, who has made both one, and has broken down the middle wall of division between us."

Ephesians 2:14

(See also John 14:27; Colossians 1:20.)

5. OUR LIFE

"When Christ who is our life appears, then you also will appear with Him in glory." Colossians 3:4

(See also John 10:10; 14:6.)

6. OUR HOPE

"Paul, an apostle of Jesus Christ, by the commandment of God our Savior and the Lord Jesus Christ, our hope."

1 Timothy 1:1

(See also Colossians 1:27; Titus 2:13; Hebrews 6:19–20.)

7. OUR LORD

"Grace, mercy, and peace from God the Father and Christ Jesus our Lord." 2 Timothy 1:2

(See also John 20:28; Acts 2:36; 1 Timothy 1:12.)

PART NINE

THE CHRISTIAN LIFE

1. THE RESOURCES OF THE CHRISTIAN

2. THE CHRIST LIFE

3. PAUL'S PLEAS

4. WHAT CHRISTIANS WERE

5. WHAT CHRISTIANS HAVE

6. WHAT CHRISTIANS KNOW

7. WHAT CHRISTIANS SHOULD DO

8. WHAT CHRISTIANS SHALL BE

9. SIX KINDS OF FRUIT

10. THE POWER OF SATAN

11. THE CHRISTIAN'S WALK

THE RESOURCES OF THE CHRISTIAN

"For in Him dwells all the fullness of the Godhead bodily."
— Colossians 2:9 —

1. THE LORD JESUS CHRIST IS OUR SALVATION.

"When the parents brought in the Child Jesus, to do for Him according to the custom of the law, he took Him up in his arms and blessed God and said, 'Lord, now You are letting Your servant depart in peace, according to Your word; for my eyes have seen Your salvation.'" Luke 2:27–30

2. THE LORD JESUS CHRIST IS OUR LIFE.

"When Christ who is our life appears, then you also will appear with Him in glory." Colossians 3:4

(See also 1 John 5:12.)

3. THE LORD JESUS CHRIST IS OUR PASSOVER.

"For indeed Christ, our Passover, was sacrificed for us."
1 Corinthians 5:7

4. THE LORD JESUS CHRIST IS OUR PEACE.

"But now in Christ Jesus you who once were far off have been made near by the blood of Christ. For He Himself is our peace."
Ephesians 2:13–14

(See also Colossians 1:20.)

5. THE LORD JESUS CHRIST IS OUR WISDOM AND RIGHTEOUSNESS.

"But of Him you are in Christ Jesus, who became for us wisdom from God—and righteousness and sanctification and redemption." 1 Corinthians 1:30

6. THE LORD JESUS CHRIST IS OUR STRENGTH.

"I can do all things through Christ who strengthens me."

Philippians 4:13

(See also Ephesians 6:10.)

7. THE LORD JESUS CHRIST IS OUR VICTORY.

"But thanks be to God, who gives us the victory through our Lord Jesus Christ." 1 Corinthians 15:57

(See also Romans 8:37.)

THE CHRIST LIFE

"For to me, to live is Christ, and to die is gain."
— Philippians 1:21 —

1. A LIFE OF OBEDIENCE
"Then He said, 'Behold, I come to do Your will, O God.'"
Hebrews 10:9
(See also Acts 9:6.)

2. A LIFE OF SERVICE
"Jesus of Nazareth . . . who went about doing good and healing all who were oppressed by the devil, for God was with Him." Acts 10:38

3. A LIFE OF POWER
"Then Jesus came and spoke to them, saying, 'All authority has been given to Me in heaven and on earth.'" Matthew 28:18
(See also Matthew 26:52–53.)

4. A LIFE OF SACRIFICE
"'Greater love has no one than this, than to lay down one's life for his friends.'" John 15:13
(See also Philippians 3:7.)

5. A LIFE OF SEPARATION
"Do not be unequally yoked together with unbelievers."
2 Corinthians 6:14

6. A LIFE OF SUFFERING
"Always carrying about in the body the dying of the Lord Jesus, that the life of Jesus also may be manifested in our body. For we who live are always delivered to death for Jesus' sake, that the life of Jesus also may be made manifested in our mortal flesh." 2 Corinthians 4:10–11

7. A LIFE OF VICTORY

"Therefore God also has highly exalted Him and given Him the name which is above every name." Philippians 2:9

"But thanks be to God, who gives us the victory through our Lord Jesus Christ." 1 Corinthians 15:57

(See also Romans 8:37; Philippians 2:10–11.)

PAUL'S PLEAS

"Now I, Paul, myself am pleading with you by the meekness and gentleness of Christ."
— 2 Corinthians 10:1 —

1. THAT YOU STRIVE TOGETHER IN PRAYER
"Now I beg you, brethren, through the Lord Jesus Christ, and through the love of the Spirit, that you strive together with me in your prayers to God for me." Romans 15:30

2. THAT YOU PRESENT YOUR BODIES A LIVING SACRIFICE
"I beseech you therefore, brethren, by the mercies of God, that you present your bodies a living sacrifice, holy, acceptable to God, which is your reasonable service." Romans 12:1

3. THAT YOU BE PERFECTLY JOINED IN ONE MIND
"Now I plead with you, brethren, by the name of our Lord Jesus Christ, that you all speak the same thing, and that there be no divisions among you, but that you be perfectly joined together in the same mind and in the same judgment."
1 Corinthians 1:10

4. THAT YOU RECEIVE NOT THE GRACE OF GOD IN VAIN
"We then, as workers together with Him also plead with you not to receive the grace of God in vain." 2 Corinthians 6:1

5. THAT YOU WALK WORTHY OF THE CALLING
"I, therefore, the prisoner of the Lord, beseech you to have a walk worthy of the calling with which you were called."
Ephesians 4:1

6. THAT YOU BE NOT SHAKEN

"Now, brethren, concerning the coming of our Lord Jesus Christ and our gathering together to Him, we ask you, not to be soon shaken in mind or troubled, either by spirit or by word or by letter, as if from us, as though the day of Christ had come." 2 Thessalonians 2:1–2

7. THAT YOU INCREASE MORE AND MORE

"We urge and exhort in the Lord Jesus that you should abound more and more, just as you received from us how you ought to walk and to please God; . . . We urge you, brethren, that you increase more and more." 1 Thessalonians 4:1, 10

WHAT CHRISTIANS WERE

"Therefore if the Son makes you free, you shall be free indeed."
— John 8:36 —

1. SLAVES

"Even so we, when we were children, were in bondage under the elements of the world." Galatians 4:3

(See also Romans 6:17, 20; Hebrews 2:15.)

2. SINNERS

"But God demonstrates His own love toward us, in that while we were still sinners, Christ died for us." Romans 5:8

(See also Romans 3:23; 5:19.)

3. DEAD IN SINS

"And you He made alive, who were dead in trespasses and sins . . . Even when we were dead in trespasses, made us alive together with Christ (by grace you have been saved)."

Ephesians 2:1, 5

4. GUILTY BEFORE GOD

"Now we know that whatever the law says, it says to those who are under the law, that every mouth may be stopped, and all the world may become guilty before God." Romans 3:19

5. ENEMIES OF GOD

"For if when we were enemies we were reconciled to God through the death of His Son, much more, having been reconciled, we shall be saved by His life." Romans 5:10

(See also Romans 5:19; Colossians 1:21.)

6. WITHOUT GOD AND WITHOUT CHRIST

"That at that time you were without Christ, being aliens from the commonwealth of Israel and strangers from the covenants of promise, having no hope and without God in the world." Ephesians 2:12

(See also Romans 9:25.)

7. FAR OFF

"But now in Christ Jesus you who were once far off have been made near by the blood of Christ." Ephesians 2:13

8. SHEEP GOING ASTRAY

"For you were like sheep going astray, but have now returned to the Shepherd and Overseer of your souls." 1 Peter 2:25

(See also Isaiah 53:6.)

9. WITHOUT STRENGTH

"For when we were still without strength, in due time Christ died for the ungodly." Romans 5:6

10. UTTERLY CORRUPT

"For we ourselves were also once foolish, disobedient, deceived, serving various lusts and pleasures, living in malice and envy, hateful and hating one another." Titus 3:3

11. CHILDREN OF WRATH

"Among whom also we all once conducted ourselves in the lusts of our flesh, fulfilling the desires of the flesh and of the mind, and were by nature children of wrath, just as the others." Ephesians 2:3

12. UNDER THE POWER OF SATAN

"In which you once walked according to the course of this world, according to the prince of the power of the air, the spirit who now works in the sons of disobedience."

Ephesians 2:2

WHAT CHRISTIANS HAVE

"And you are complete in Him."

— Colossians 2:10 —

1. CHRIST JESUS
"As you have therefore received Christ Jesus the Lord, so walk in Him." Colossians 2:6

2. HOLY SPIRIT
"Do you not know that you are the temple of God and that the Spirit of God dwells in you?" 1 Corinthians 3:16

(See also Acts 10:47; 1 Corinthians 6:19.)

3. REDEMPTION
"In Him we have redemption through His blood, the forgiveness of sins, according to the riches of His grace."
Ephesians 1:7

4. ETERNAL LIFE
"These things have I written to you who believe in the name of the Son of God, that you may know that you have eternal life, and that you may continue to believe in the name of the Son of God." 1 John 5:13

5. AN ADVOCATE
"And if anyone sins, we have an Advocate with the Father, Jesus Christ the righteous." 1 John 2:1

6. A HIGH PRIEST
"Seeing then that we have a great High Priest who has passed through the heavens, Jesus the Son of God, let us hold fast our confession." Hebrews 4:14

(See also Hebrews 8:1.)

7. ACCESS TO GOD

"For through Him we both have access by one Spirit to the Father." Ephesians 2:18

(See also Romans 5:1–2.)

WHAT CHRISTIANS KNOW

"The Lord give you understanding in all things."

— 2 Timothy 2:7 —

1. THAT THE SON OF GOD HAS COME

"And we know that the Son of God has come and has given us an understanding, that we may know Him who is true; and we are in Him who is true, in His Son Jesus Christ." 1 John 5:20

2. THAT THEY HAVE PASSED FROM DEATH TO LIFE

"We know that we have passed from death to life, because we love the brethren. He who does not love his brother abides in death." 1 John 3:14

3. THAT THEY ARE OF GOD

"We know that we are of God, and the whole world lies under the sway of the wicked one." 1 John 5:19

4. THAT GOD ABIDES IN THEM

"And by this we know that He abides in us, by the Spirit whom He has given us." 1 John 3:24

5. THAT ALL THINGS WORK TOGETHER FOR GOOD

"And we know that all things work together for good to those who love God, to those who are the called according to His purpose." Romans 8:28

6. THAT THE WHOLE CREATION LIVES IN PAIN

"For we know that the whole creation groans and labors with birth pangs together until now." Romans 8:22

7. THAT THEY HAVE A BUILDING OF GOD

"For we know that if our earthly house, this tent, is destroyed, we have a building from God, a house not made with hands, eternal in the heavens." 2 Corinthians 5:1

WHAT CHRISTIANS SHOULD DO

"And whatever you do, do it heartily, as to the Lord."
~ Colossians 3:23 ~

1. BELIEVE ON GOD'S SON.
"And this is His commandment: that we should believe on the name of His Son Jesus Christ and love one another, as He gave us commandment." 1 John 3:23

2. WALK IN NEWNESS OF LIFE.
"Therefore we were buried with Him through baptism into death, that just as Christ was raised from the dead by the glory of the Father, even so we also should walk in newness of life." Romans 6:4

3. LIVE UNTO RIGHTEOUSNESS.
"Who Himself bore our sins in His own body on the tree, that we, having died to sins, might live for righteousness— by whose stripes you were healed." 1 Peter 2:24

4. LOVE ONE ANOTHER.
"For this is the message that you heard from the beginning, that we should love one another." 1 John 3:11

(See also John 15:12.)

5. SHOW FORTH HIS PRAISES.
"But you are a chosen generation, a royal priesthood, a holy nation, His own special people, that you may proclaim the praises of Him who called you out of darkness into His marvelous light." 1 Peter 2:9

6. CONTEND FOR THE FAITH.

"Beloved, while I was very diligent to write to you concerning our common salvation, I found it necessary to write to you exhorting you to contend earnestly for the faith which was once for all delivered to the saints." Jude 3

7. BRING FORTH FRUIT.

"That you may have a walk worthy of the Lord, fully pleasing Him, being fruitful in every good work and increasing in the knowledge of God." Colossians 1:10

(See also John 15:8; Romans 7:4.)

WHAT CHRISTIANS SHALL BE

"'Eye has not seen, nor ear heard . . . the things which God has prepared for those who love Him.'"

1 Corinthians 2:9

1. THEY SHALL BE CHANGED.

"Behold, I tell you a mystery: We shall not all sleep, but we shall all be changed—in a moment, in the twinkling of an eye, at the last trumpet. For the trumpet will sound, and the dead will be raised incorruptible, and we shall be changed."

1 Corinthians 15:51–52

2. THEY SHALL BE CAUGHT UP.

"Then we who are alive and remain shall be caught up together with them in the clouds to meet the Lord in the air. And thus we shall always be with the Lord."

1 Thessalonians 4:17

3. THEY SHALL BE LIKE CHRIST.

"Beloved, now we are children of God; and it has not yet been revealed what we shall be, but we know that when He is revealed, we shall be like Him, for we shall see Him as He is."

1 John 3:2

4. THEY SHALL APPEAR WITH CHRIST.

"When Christ who is our life appears, then you also will appear with Him in glory." Colossians 3:4

5. THEY SHALL BE JUDGES.

"Do you not know that the saints shall judge the world? . . . Do you not know that we shall judge angels?"

1 Corinthians 6:2–3

6. THEY SHALL BE PRIESTS.

"Blessed and holy is he who has part in the first resurrection.
Over such the second death has no power, but they shall be
priests of God and of Christ, and shall reign with Him a
thousand years." Revelation 20:6

(See also Revelation 1:6; 5:10.)

7. THEY SHALL BE WITH CHRIST FOREVER.

"And thus we shall always be with the Lord. Therefore
comfort one another with these words." 1 Thessalonians 4:17–18

SIX KINDS OF FRUIT

"By this My Father is glorified, that you bear much fruit."
— John 15:8 —

1. GOOD FRUIT
"'Every tree that does not bear good fruit is cut down and thrown into the fire.'" Matthew 7:19

2. BAD FRUIT
"'Even so, every good tree bears good fruit, but a bad tree bears bad fruit.'" Matthew 7:17

(See also Matthew 12:33.)

3. MUCH FRUIT
"'Verily, verily, I say unto you, unless a corn of wheat falls into the ground and die, it abideth alone: but if it die, it bringeth forth much fruit.'" John 12:24 (KJV)

4. MORE FRUIT
"'Every branch in Me that does not bear fruit He takes away; and every branch that bears fruit He prunes, that it may bear more fruit.'" John 15:2

5. PEACEABLE FRUIT
"Now no chastening seems to be joyful for the present , but grievous; nevertheless, afterward it yields the peaceable fruit of righteousness to those who have been trained by it."

Hebrews 12:11

6. PRECIOUS FRUIT
"Therefore be patient, brethren, until the coming of the Lord. See how the farmer waits for the precious fruit of the earth, waiting patiently for it until it receives the early and latter rain." James 5:7

THE POWER OF SATAN

"Then Satan went out from the presence of the Lord."
— Job 1:12 —

1. SATAN HAS POWER TO TEMPT.
"And He was there in the wilderness forty days, tempted by Satan." Mark 1:13

2. SATAN HAS POWER TO HINDER.
"Therefore we wanted to come to you—even I, Paul, time and again—but Satan hindered us." 1 Thessalonians 2:18

3. SATAN HAS POWER TO ENSNARE.
"Moreover he must have a good testimony among those who are outside, lest he fall into reproach and the snare of the devil." 1 Timothy 3:7

(See also 2 Timothy 2:24–26.)

4. SATAN HAS POWER TO ACCUSE.
"Then I heard a loud voice saying in heaven, 'Now salvation, and strength, and the kingdom of our God, and the power of His Christ have come, for the accuser of our brethren, who accused them before our God day and night, has been cast down." Revelation 12:10

(See also Job 1:6–11.)

5. SATAN HAS POWER TO OPPOSE.
"Then he showed me Joshua the high priest standing before the Angel of the Lord, and Satan standing at his right hand to oppose him." Zechariah 3:1

6. SATAN HAS POWER TO DECEIVE.
"And the Lord God said to the woman, 'What is this you have done?' And the woman said, 'The serpent deceived me, and I ate.'" Genesis 3:13

7. SATAN HAS POWER TO WORK WONDERS.

"The coming of the lawless one is according to the working of Satan, with all power, signs, and lying wonders."

2 Thessalonians 2:9

(See also Revelation 16:14.)

8. SATAN HAS POWER TO INFLICT DISEASE.

"Then Satan went out from the presence of the Lord, and struck Job with painful boils from the sole of his foot to the crown of his head." Job 2:7

9. SATAN HAS POWER TO BIND.

"'So ought not this woman, being a daughter of Abraham, whom Satan has bound—think of it—for eighteen years, be loosed from this bond on the Sabbath?'" Luke 13:16

10. SATAN HAS POWER TO PERSECUTE.

"Now when the dragon [the devil] saw that he had been cast to the earth, he persecuted the woman who gave birth to the male Child." Revelation 12:13

(See also Job 1:7; Luke 22:31–32.)

11. SATAN HAS POWER TO DESTROY.

"'The thief does not come except to steal, and to kill, and to destroy.'" John 10:10

(See also Hebrews 2:14.)

12. SATAN HAS POWER TO DEVOUR.

"Be sober, be vigilant; because your adversary the devil walks about like a roaring lion, seeking whom he may devour. Resist him, steadfast in the faith. " 1 Peter 5:8–9

13. OUR BLESSED DELIVERER

"He who sins is of the devil, for the devil has sinned from the beginning. For this purpose the Son of God was manifested, that He might destroy the works of the devil." 1 John 3:8

THE CHRISTIAN'S WALK

"Blessed are the undefiled in the way, who walk in the law of the Lord!"
— Psalm 119:1 —

1. WALK IN NEWNESS OF LIFE.

"Therefore we were buried with Him through baptism into death, that just as Christ was raised from the dead by the glory of the Father, even so we also should walk in newness of life." Romans 6:4

2. WALK IN GOOD WORKS.

"For we are His workmanship, created in Christ Jesus for good works, which God prepared beforehand that we should walk in them." Ephesians 2:10

3. WALK IN LOVE.

"And walk in love, as Christ also has loved us and given Himself for us, an offering and a sacrifice to God for a sweet-smelling aroma." Ephesians 5:2

4. WALK IN THE SPIRIT.

"I say then: Walk in the Spirit, and you shall not fulfill the lust of the flesh." Galatians 5:16

5. WALK IN HIM.

"As you have therefore received Christ Jesus the Lord, so walk in Him, rooted and built up in Him and established in the faith." Colossians 2:6

6. WALK IN WISDOM.

"Walk in wisdom toward those who are outside, redeeming the time. Let your speech always be with grace, seasoned with salt, that you may know how you ought to answer each one." Colossians 4:5

7. WALK IN LIGHT.

"But if we walk in the light as He is in the light, we have fellowship with one another, and the blood of Jesus Christ His Son cleanses us from all sin." 1 John 1:7

8. WALK WORTHILY.

"I, therefore, the prisoner of the Lord, beseech you to have a walk worthy of the calling with which you were called."

Ephesians 4:1

PART TEN

THE CHRISTIAN'S HEART

1. REJOICE

2. ATTITUDES OF THE MIND

3. FREE INDEED

4. THE HOPE OF THE RESURRECTION

5. WHAT CHRISTIANS SHOULD BE

REJOICE

"Rejoice in the Lord always. Again I will say, rejoice!"
— Philippians 4:4 —

R— REJOICE IN THE LORD, THE REDEEMER.
"In whom we have redemption through His blood, the forgiveness of sins." Colossians 1:14

E— REJOICE IN THE LORD, THE ETERNAL ONE.
"And His name will be called Wonderful, Counselor, Mighty God, Everlasting Father, Prince of Peace." Isaiah 9:6

J— REJOICE IN THE LORD, THE JUST ONE.
"'Rejoice greatly, O daughter of Zion! Shout, O daughter of Jerusalem! Behold, your King is coming to you; He is just and having salvation.'" Zechariah 9:9

O—REJOICE IN THE LORD, THE OMNIPOTENT ONE.
"Then Jesus came and spoke to them, saying, 'All authority has been given to Me in heaven and on earth.'" Matthew 28:18

I— REJOICE IN THE LORD, THE INTERCESSOR.
"Therefore He is also able to save to the uttermost those who come to God through Him, since He ever lives to make intercession for them." Hebrews 7:25

C—REJOICE IN THE LORD, THE COMING ONE.
"And if I go and prepare a place for you, I will come again and receive you to Myself; that where I am, there you may be also." John 14:3

E— REJOICE IN THE LORD, THE ENCOURAGING ONE.
"'Be of good cheer! It is I; do not be afraid.'" Matthew 14:27

ATTITUDES OF THE MIND

"Set your mind on things above."
~ Colossians 3:2 ~

1. THE HUMILITY OF THE MIND
"Therefore, as the elect of God, holy and beloved, put on tender mercies, kindness, humbleness of mind, meekness, longsuffering." Colossians 3:12

(See also Acts 20:19; Philippians 2:3.)

2. THE LOINS OF THE MIND
"Therefore gird up the loins of your mind, be sober, and rest your hope fully upon the grace that is to be brought unto you at the revelation of Jesus Christ." 1 Peter 1:13

3. THE FOCUS OF THE MIND
"Seek those things which are above, where Christ is, sitting at the right hand of God. Set your mind on things above, not on things on the earth. For you died, and your life is hidden with Christ in God." Colossians 3:1–3

4. THE RENEWING OF THE MIND
"And do not be conformed to this world, but be transformed by the renewing of your mind, that you may prove what is that good and acceptable and perfect will of God."

Romans 12:2

FREE INDEED

"'Therefore if the Son makes you free, you shall be free indeed.'"
— John 8:36 —

1. FREE FROM THE LAW
"But now we have been delivered from the law, . . . that we should serve in the newness of the Spirit." Romans 7:6

(See also Romans 6:14; Galatians 5:18.)

2. FREE FROM THE CURSE
"Christ has redeemed us from the curse of the law, having become a curse for us (for it is written, 'Cursed is everyone who hangs on a tree.')" Galatians 3:13

3. FREE FROM SIN
"Knowing this, that our old man was crucified with Him, that the body of sin might be done away with, that we should no longer be slaves of sin. For he who has died has been freed from sin." Romans 6:6–7

(See also Romans 6:11, 22; 8:2.)

4. FREE FROM CONDEMNATION
"There is therefore now no condemnation to those who are in Christ Jesus." Romans 8:1

5. FREE FROM SATAN'S POWER
"We know that whoever is born of God does not sin; but he who has been born of God keeps himself, and the wicked one does not touch him." 1 John 5:18

(See also Acts 26:18.)

6. FREE FROM DEATH

"'And whoever lives and believes in Me shall never die.'"

John 11:26

"Who delivered us from so great a death, and does deliver us;
in whom we trust that He will still deliver us."

2 Corinthians 1:10

7. FREE FROM HELL

"Jesus . . . delivers us from the wrath to come."

1 Thessalonians 1:10

"'I am He who lives, and was dead, and behold, I am alive
forevermore. Amen. And I have the keys of Hades and of
Death.'" Revelation 1:18

THE HOPE OF THE RESURRECTION

"Looking for the blessed hope."
— Titus 2:13 —

1. THE RESURRECTION IS A LIVING HOPE.

"Blessed be the God and Father of our Lord Jesus Christ, who according to His abundant mercy has begotten us again to a living hope through the resurrection of Jesus Christ from the dead." 1 Peter 1:3

2. THE RESURRECTION IS A SURE HOPE.

"This hope we have as an anchor of the soul, both sure and steadfast, and which enters the Presence behind the veil, where the forerunner has entered for us, even Jesus, having become High Priest forever according to the order of Melchizdek." Hebrews 6:19–20

(See also Revelation 1:18.)

3. THE RESURRECTION IS A PURIFYING HOPE.

"Beloved, now we are children of God; and it has not yet been revealed what we shall be, but we know that when He is revealed, we shall be like Him, for we shall see Him as He is. And everyone who has this hope in Him purifies himself, just as He is pure." 1 John 3:2–3

4. THE RESURRECTION IS A COMFORTING HOPE.

"The dead in Christ will rise first. Then we who are alive and remain shall be caught up together with them in the clouds to meet the Lord in the air. And thus we shall always be with the Lord. Therefore comfort one another with these words."

1 Thessalonians 4:16–18

5. THE RESURRECTION IS A SUSTAINING HOPE.

"For I consider that the sufferings of this present time are not worthy to be compared with the glory which shall be revealed in us." Romans 8:18

(See also Romans 5:1-3; 2 Corinthians 4:17–18.)

6. THE RESURRECTION IS A SATISFYING HOPE.

"As for me, I will see Your face in righteousness; I shall be satisfied when I awake in Your likeness." Psalm 17:15

7. THE RESURRECTION IS A BLESSED HOPE.

"Blessed and holy is he who has part in the first resurrection. Over such the second death has no power, but they shall be priests of God and of Christ, and shall reign with Him a thousand years." Revelation 20:6

(See also Titus 2:13.)

WHAT CHRISTIANS SHOULD BE

"Working in you what is well pleasing in His sight."

Hebrews 13:21

1. FRUITFUL

"Therefore, my brethren, you also have become dead to the law through the body of Christ, that you may be married to another, even to Him who was raised from the dead, that we should bear fruit to God." Romans 7:4

2. THANKFUL

"And let the peace of God rule in your hearts, to which also you were called in one body; and be thankful."

Colossians 3:15

(See also Ephesians 5:20.)

3. CONTENTED

"And be content with such things as you have. For He Himself has said, 'I will never leave you nor forsake you.'" Hebrews 13:5

4. EXAMPLES

"Let no one despise your youth, but be an example to the believers in word, in conduct, in love, in spirit, in faith, in purity." 1 Timothy 4:12

5. TRANSFORMED

"And do not be conformed to this world, but be transformed by the renewing of your mind, that you may prove what is that good and acceptable and perfect will of God."

Romans 12:2

PART ELEVEN

PRAYER

1. HOW TO PRAY
2. CONDITIONS OF ACCEPTABLE PRAYER
3. WHY PRAYERS ARE NOT HEARD

HOW TO PRAY

"Men always ought to pray and not lose heart."

⌒~ Luke 18:1 ~⌒

1. WITH THE HEART

"'Then you will call upon Me and go and pray to Me, and I
will listen to you. And you will seek Me and find Me when
you search for Me with all your heart.'" Jeremiah 29:12–13

(See also Psalms 119:58; 145.)

2. WITH A TRUE HEART

"Let us draw near with a true heart in full assurance of faith,
having our hearts sprinkled from an evil conscience."

Hebrews 10:22

3. WITH PREPARATION OF HEART

"'If you would prepare your heart, and stretch out your hands
toward Him.'" Job 11:13

4. WITH THE SPIRIT OF UNDERSTANDING

"I will pray with the spirit, and I will also pray with the
understanding." 1 Corinthians 14:15

5. WITH CONFIDENCE IN GOD

"When I cry out to You, then my enemies will turn back; this
I know, because God is for me." Psalm 56:9

(See also Psalm 86:7; Hebrews 4:16; 1 John 5:14.)

6. WITH HUMILITY

"'If My people who are called by My name will humble
themselves, and pray and seek My face, and turn from their
wicked ways, then will I hear from heaven, and will forgive
their sin and heal their land.'" 2 Chronicles 7:14

(See also 2 Chronicles 33:12; Psalm 10:17.)

7. WITH EARNESTNESS AND IMPORTUNITY
"The effective, fervent prayer of a righteous man avails much. Elijah was a man with a nature like ours, and he prayed earnestly that it would not rain; and it did not rain on the land for three years and six months." James 5:16–17

(See also Genesis 32:26; Luke 11:8–9.)

8. WITH SUBMISSION TO GOD
"And He was withdrawn from them about a stone's throw, and He knelt down and prayed, saying, 'Father, if it is Your will, remove this cup from Me; nevertheless not My will, but Yours, be done.'" Luke 22:41–42

9. WITH ASSURANCE OF FAITH
"'Call to Me, and I will answer you, and show you great and mighty things, which you do not know.'" Jeremiah 33:3

(See also Mark 11:22–24; Psalm 50:15.)

10. WITH THANKSGIVING
"Be anxious for nothing, but in everything by prayer and supplication, with thanksgiving, let your requests be made known to God; and the peace of God, which surpasses all understanding, will guard your hearts and minds through Christ Jesus." Philippians 4:6–7

(See also 1 Thessalonians 5:18.)

CONDITIONS OF ACCEPTABLE PRAYER

"'If you abide in Me, and My words abide in you, . . . it shall be done for you'"

⁓ John 15:7 ⁓

1. IN THE NAME OF JESUS

"'Most assuredly, I say to you, whatever you ask the Father in My name He will give you.'" John 16:23

(See also John 14:13–14; 15:16.)

2. IN FAITH

"'And all things, whatever you ask in prayer, believing, you will receive.'" Matthew 21:22

(See also James 1:6; 5:15.)

3. IN SINCERITY

"'If My people who are called by My name will humble themselves, and pray and seek My face, and turn from their wicked ways, then I will hear from heaven, and will forgive their sin and heal their land.'" 2 Chronicles 7:14

4. IN RIGHTEOUSNESS

"'For the eyes of the Lord are on the righteous, and his ears are open to their prayers; but the face of the Lord is against those who do evil.'" 1 Peter 3:12

(See also 1 John 3:22; Psalm 34:15.)

5. IN HUMILITY

"'And the tax collector, standing afar off, would not so much as raise his eyes to heaven, but beat his breast, saying, "God be merciful to me a sinner!" I tell you, this man went down to his house justified rather than the other; for everyone who exalts himself will be abased, and he who humbles himself will be exalted.'" Luke 18:13–14

6.WITH FORGIVENESS
"'And whenever you stand praying, if you have anything against anyone, forgive him, that your Father in heaven may also forgive you your trespasses.'" Mark 11:25

(See also Ephesians 4:30–32.)

7. WITH PERSEVERANCE
"'I say to you, though he will not rise and give to him because he is his friend, yet because of his persistence he will rise and give him as many as he needs. And I say to you, ask, and it will be given to you; seek, and you will find; knock, and it will be opened to you.'" Luke 11:8–9

(See also Luke 18:1-8; Ephesians 6:18.)

WHY PRAYERS ARE NOT HEARD

"O My God, I cry in the daytime, but You do not hear."

~ Psalm 22:2 ~

1. UNJUDGED SIN

"Behold, the Lord's hand is not shortened, that it cannot save; nor His ear heavy, that it cannot hear. But your iniquities have separated you from your God; and your sins have hidden His face from you, so that He will not hear." Isaiah 59:1–2

(See also Psalm 66:18; Isaiah 1:15.)

2. UNBELIEF

"But let him ask in faith, with no doubting, for he who doubts is like a wave of the sea driven and tossed by the wind." James 1:6

(See also Matthew 21:22; Hebrews 11:6.)

3. LOVE OF PLEASURE

"You ask and do not receive, because you ask amiss, that you may spend it on your pleasures." James 4:3

4. PRIDE

"'There they cry out, but He does not answer, because of the pride of evil men.'" Job 35:12

(See also Psalm 138:6; James 4:6.)

5. INDIFFERENCE

"Then he said, 'Take the arrows; so he took them'. And he said to the king of Israel, 'Strike the ground'; so he struck three times, and stopped. And the man of God was angry with him, and said, 'You should have struck five or six times.'"

2 Kings 13:18–19

(See also Luke 11:5–9; 18:1–7.)

6. AN UNFORGIVING SPIRIT
"'And whenever you stand praying, if you have anything against anyone, forgive him.'" Mark 11:25

(See also Ephesians 4:32.)

7. NEGLECT OF GOD'S WORD
"One who turns away his ear from hearing the law, even his prayer shall be an abomination." Proverbs 28:9

PART TWELVE

THE RETURN OF CHRIST

1. LAST DAYS

2. THE SECOND COMING OF CHRIST

3. THE PURPOSE OF CHRIST'S SECOND COMING

4. THE MANNER OF THE SECOND COMING

5. THE SAINTS AND THE SECOND COMING

6. THE CROWNS OF THE BIBLE

LAST DAYS

"Then comes the end."

— 1 Corinthians 15:24 —

1. GOD SPEAKS BY HIS SON.

"God, who at various times and in different ways spoke in time past to the fathers by the prophets, has in these last days spoken to us by His Son." Hebrews 1:1–2

2. GOD POURS OUT HIS SPIRIT.

"'And it shall come to pass in the last days, says God, that I will pour out of My Spirit on all flesh; your sons and your daughters shall prophesy, your young men shall see visions, your old men shall dream dreams.'" Acts 2:17

3. GOD MAKES KNOWN WHAT SHALL BE.

"'But there is a God in heaven who reveals secrets, and He has made known to King Nebuchadnezzar what will be in the latter days.'" Daniel 2:28

4. PERILOUS TIMES WILL COME.

"In the last days perilous times will come." 2 Timothy 3:1

(See also 2 Timothy 3: 2–5, 12.)

5. SCOFFERS WILL COME.

"Knowing this first: that scoffers will come in the last days, walking according to their own lusts, and saying, 'Where is the promise of His coming? For since the fathers fell asleep, all things continue as they were from the beginning of creation.'" 2 Peter 3:3–4

6. THE FUTURE KINGDOM WILL BE ESTABLISHED.

"Now it shall come to pass in the latter days that the mountain of the Lord's house shall be established on the top of the mountains, and shall be exalted above the hills; and all nations shall flow to it." Isaiah 2:2

THE SECOND COMING OF CHRIST

" 'This same Jesus . . . will so come in like manner."
~ Acts 1:11 ~

1. THE SECOND COMING WILL BRING THE LAST TIME.

"Who are kept by the power of God through faith for salvation ready to be revealed in the last time." 1 Peter 1:5

2. THE SECOND COMING WILL BRING TIMES OF RESTORATION.

"Whom heaven must receive until the times of restoration of all things, which God has spoken by the mouth of all His holy prophets since the world began." Acts 3:21

3. THE SECOND COMING WILL BRING TIMES OF REFRESHING.

"'Repent therefore and be converted, that your sins may be blotted out, so that times of refreshing may come from the presence of the Lord.'" Acts 3:19

4. THE SECOND COMING WILL BRING CHRIST'S APPEARANCE.

"That the genuineness of your faith, being much more precious than gold that perishes, though it is tested by fire, may be found to praise, honor, and glory at the revelation of Jesus Christ." 1 Peter 1:7

(See also Titus 2:13; 1 Peter 1:13.)

5. THE SECOND COMING WILL BRING THE DAY OF OUR LORD JESUS CHRIST.

"Who will also confirm you to the end, that you may be blameless in the day of our Lord Jesus Christ."

1 Corinthians 1:8

(See also 2 Peter 3:10.)

6. THE SECOND COMING WILL BRING THE DAY OF GOD.

"Looking for and hastening the coming of the day of God, because of which the heavens will be dissolved being on fire, and the elements will melt with fervent heat." 2 Peter 3:12

THE PURPOSE OF CHRIST'S SECOND COMING

"'Where is He who has been born King of the Jews?'"

⌐— Matthew 2:2 —⌐

HE IS COMING:

1. TO COMPLETE THE SALVATION OF THE SAINTS

"So Christ was offered once to bear the sins of many. To those who eagerly wait for Him He will appear a second time, apart from sin, for salvation." Hebrews 9:28

(See also Philippians 3:20–21; 1 Peter 1:5.)

2. TO BE GLORIFIED IN HIS SAINTS

"When He comes . . . to be glorified in His saints."

2 Thessalonians 1:10

3. TO BE ADMIRED BY THOSE WHO BELIEVE

"When He comes to . . . to be admired among all those who believe." 2 Thessalonians 1:10

4. TO BRING TO LIGHT THE HIDDEN THINGS OF DARKNESS

"Therefore judge nothing before the time, until the Lord comes, who will both bring to light the hidden things of darkness and reveal the counsels of the hearts."

1 Corinthians 4:5

5. TO JUDGE ALL MEN

"'For the Father judges no one, but has committed all judgment to the Son.'" John 5:22

(See also 2 Timothy 4:1; Jude 14, 15; Revelation 20:11–13.)

6. TO DESTROY DEATH

"For He must reign till He has put all enemies under His feet. The last enemy that will be destroyed is death."

1 Corinthians 15:25–26

7. TO REIGN AS KING

"'The kingdoms of this world have become the kingdoms of our Lord and of His Christ, and He shall reign forever and ever!'" Revelation 11:15

(See also Isaiah 24:23; Daniel 7:14.)

THE MANNER OF THE SECOND COMING

"He who testifies to these things says, 'Surely I am coming quickly.'"
— Revelation 22:20 —

CHRIST IS COMING:

1. ON THE CLOUDS
"'And they will see the Son of Man coming on the clouds of heaven.'" Matthew 24:30

(See also Matthew 26:64; Revelation 1:7.)

2. IN THE GLORY OF HIS FATHER
"'For the Son of Man will come in the glory of His Father.'"
Matthew 16:27

3. IN HIS OWN GLORY
"'When the Son of Man comes in His glory.'" Matthew 25:31

4. IN FLAMING FIRE
"And to give you who are troubled rest with us when the Lord Jesus is revealed from heaven with His mighty angels, in flaming fire taking vengeance on those who do not know God, and on those who do not obey the gospel of our Lord Jesus Christ." 2 Thessalonians 1:7–8

5. WITH GREAT POWER
"'And they will see the Son of Man coming on the clouds of heaven with power and great glory.'" Matthew 24:30

6. WITH HIS ANGELS
"'For the Son of Man will come in the glory of His Father with His angels.'" Matthew 16:27

7. WITH A SHOUT
"For the Lord Himself will descend from heaven with a shout, with the voice of an archangel, and with the trumpet of God."
1 Thessalonians 4:16

8. WITH HIS SAINTS
"And may the Lord make you increase and abound in love to one another and to all, just as we do you, so that He may establish your hearts blameless in holiness before our God and Father at the coming of our Lord Jesus Christ with all His saints." 1 Thessalonians 3:12–13

9. SUDDENLY
"'Lest, coming suddenly, he find you sleeping.'" Mark 13:36
(See also Matthew 24:27; Revelation 22:20.)

10. UNEXPECTEDLY
"'Watch therefore, for you know neither the day nor the hour in which the Son of Man is coming.'" Matthew 25:13
(See also Matthew 24:42, 44.)

THE SAINTS AND THE SECOND COMING

"It has not yet been revealed what we shall be, but we know . . . we shall see Him as He is."

1 John 3:2

1. THEY SHALL BE PRESERVED.

"Being confident of this very thing, that He who has begun a good work in you will complete it until the day of Jesus Christ." Philippians 1:6

(See also 2 Timothy 4:18; 1 Peter 1:5; Jude 24.)

2. THEY SHALL NOT BE ASHAMED.

"And now, little children, abide in Him, that when He appears, we may have confidence and not be ashamed before Him at His coming." 1 John 2:28

3. THEY SHALL BE BLAMELESS.

"Waiting for the revelation of our Lord Jesus Christ, who will also confirm you to the end, that you may be blameless in the day of our Lord Jesus Christ." 1 Corinthians 1:7–8

(See also 1 Thessalonians 3:13; 5:23.)

4. THEY SHALL BE LIKE HIM.

"Beloved, now are we children of God; and it has not yet been revealed what we shall be, but we know that when He is revealed, we shall be like Him." 1 John 3:2

(See also Philippians 3:20–21.)

5. THEY SHALL APPEAR WITH HIM IN GLORY.

"When Christ who is our life appears, then you also will appear with Him in glory." Colossians 3:4

6. THEY SHALL RECEIVE A CROWN OF GLORY.

"Finally, there is laid up for me the crown of righteousness, which the Lord, the righteous Judge, will give to me on that Day, and not to me only but also to all who have loved His appearing." 2 Timothy 4:8

(See also 1 Peter 5:4.)

7. THEY SHALL REIGN WITH HIM.

"If we endure, we shall also reign with Him." 2 Timothy 2:12

(See also Revelation 5:10; 20:6; 22:5.)

THE CROWNS OF THE BIBLE

"'Hold fast what you have, that no one may take your crown.'"

― Revelation 3:11 ―

1. THE CROWN OF THORNS
"When they had twisted a crown of thorns, they put it on His head, and a reed in His right hand. And they bowed the knee before Him and mocked Him, saying, 'Hail, King of the Jews!'" Matthew 27:29

2. THE CROWN OF RIGHTEOUSNESS
"Finally, there is laid up for me the crown of righteousness, which the Lord, the righteous Judge, will give to me on that Day, and not to me only but also to all who have loved His appearing." 2 Timothy 4:8

3. THE CROWN OF LIFE
"Blessed is the man who endures temptation; for when he has been proved, he will receive the crown of life which the Lord has promised to those who love Him." James 1:12

(See also Revelation 2:10).

4. THE CROWN OF REJOICING
"For what is our hope, or joy, or crown of rejoicing? Is it not even you in the presence of our Lord Jesus Christ at His coming?" 1 Thessalonians 2:19

5. THE CROWN OF GLORY
"And when the Chief Shepherd appears, you will receive the crown of glory that does not fade away." 1 Peter 5:4

(See also Isaiah 28:5).

6. THE IMPERISHABLE CROWN
"And everyone who competes for the prize is temperate in all

things. Now they do it to obtain a perishable crown, but we for an imperishable crown." 1 Corinthians 9:25

7. THE CROWN OF GOLD
"And I looked, and behold, a white cloud, and on the cloud sat One like the Son of Man, having on His head a golden crown, and in His hand a sharp sickle." Revelation 14:14

Moody Press, a ministry of Moody Bible Institute,
is designed for education, evangelization, and edification.
If we may assist you in knowing more about Christ
and the Christian life, please write us without obligation:
Moody Press, c/o MLM, Chicago, Illinois 60610.